fact book(2) .com

An Idea

MANOJ SINHA

Notion Press

No.8, 3rd Cross Street,
CIT Colony, Mylapore,
Chennai, Tamil Nadu – 600004

First Published by Notion Press 2020
Copyright © Manoj Sinha 2020
All Rights Reserved.

ISBN 978-1-63633-701-2

With the Blessings

of

My Mother

(In Tune with the Gods)

Dedicated

To

YOU

(   )

Because

I know your love is deeper now

Than what your readership says;

Without your telling me, somehow

I feel it in a hundred ways.

Contents

Postface

Liked by YOU, I am overwhelmed with love. This is a platform where a writer cannot express his gratitude except by writing his second book. I have innovated it a little bit. For this, I would like you to go back to page no 5, write your full name in bold letters and then again read the four-line stanza dedicated to YOU. For the first-time reader also, it is the same. In fact, it was not easy for a writer to be known in the writers' world, but it is you who can make him an established one.

For those who are holding my book for the first time, they can easily know that it is the second book in continuity for the second consecutive year, as the name suggests. If my previous book was an introduction, then this book carries an idea. It is a journey from facebook.com to factbook.com. All the chapters of my first book as well as of this book are posts on my home page of Facebook.

I would like to remind my readers that I had posted only those facts which were current at that time and associated it with what was on my mind. I have tried in this book to make relevancy with the present scenarios as well. The facts are either important or interesting. But one lacuna remains. While posting my write-ups on the Facebook page I used to get an immediate reaction. Some favoured it; some commented adversely. In the book-form, you just accept what is written without expressing your reaction/view, although it is generated at the same time when you read any piece of information under any chapter.

This book is introducing a feature "OVER TO YOU" on its last page. Do write down your views/comments in ink immediately when you capture it while reading any chapter in this book and send it at my mail id manojkumarsinha2002@yahoo.co.in through scanning or rewriting.

I would try my best to resolve your query and accept where I went wrong so that I can make myself more valuable to you. Even you can write to me about the information that you have or the information you want to have. Your important information, if found valuable and factual, will be published in my next book with your name and place of residence. You can even tweet me @ManojSi62843596.

I am the live example of, what you see, develops. I was born to my parents who were in teaching jobs. My paternal uncle, Arun Sinha, is a well-known newspaper editor. So, I remained in touch with the books that decorated their personal libraries. Although they were out of the syllabus for me, they developed a lot of interest in me. Now, I am part of their libraries.

I am thankful for book-fairs, especially, Delhi Book Fair that provided me the books I wanted to have. While visiting book-fairs, I had not expected myself to be on the shelves for my readers, so I am thankful to my publishers as well for providing me that opportunity.

I cannot ignore some of the family members who contributed towards it by encouraging me for this habit. My paternal aunt used to give my example to her family members. I have always found myself surrounded by my beautiful sisters, who till date are not tired of praising me.

Once again, there are no words for my confidante, my wife, Sujata Sinha. Now she has taken the additional role of controlling the publications and guiding me accordingly. My sons Utkarsh and Utkrisht have been my counsellors in efforts. While Utkarsh played the role of a motivator, Utkrisht has always proved a rescuer. I am not speaking of them with the pride of a parent; in fact, they parented me.

When my first book got published in December 2019, its arrival was contemporaneous with that of COVID-19. The lockdown caused due to it disturbed the sale of the book. To my satisfaction, the book gave the results at every point of sale. But it would have been much better, had the corona effect not been there.

Thus, when I decided to publish my second book, I decided to make it a ladder to reach you more effectively. I felt it necessary too because several myths are circulating about its existence and its cure. Lack of knowledge created myth; myth infected the mind; infected mind caused hypochondria. And moreover, how can any informative book be published this year without the topic of COVID-19 in it. That is why I deviated from my Facebook posts, and wrote the chapter "Invisible Antimen", especially for YOU.

Invisible Antimen

A virus was originally the venom of a snake and was an English borrowing of a Latin word 'virus', meaning thereby sap, slime, or ooze. This is also the source of virulent, from the same Latin source 'virulentous' which indicates 'full of sap'.

Early medical practitioners did not understand the structure and properties of the virus and used the word for a substance produced in the body as the result of the disease. The modern meaning, 'a submicroscopic organism which can cause disease' dates from the 1800s onwards.

The viruses were thought to be one of the living organisms initially. Although diseases caused by viruses have been known since the 1700s and cures for many were affected, the causative agent was not closely examined until 1892. In 1892, a Russian bacteriologist, D Ivanovski, observed that the causative agent (later proved to be a virus) of tobacco mosaic disease could pass through a porcelain filter impermeable to bacteria. In 1935, the tobacco mosaic virus became the first virus to be crystallized. (A virus 'crystal' consists of several thousand viruses).

In 1898 Dutch scientist Martinis W. Beijernick first surmised that the virus under study was a new kind of infectious agent, which he designated Contagium Vivum

Fluidum meaning that it was a live, reproducing organism that differed from other organisms like bacteria, archaea, algae, fungi, protozoans, etc.

The ongoing researches proved that the virus is devoid of a cell, unlike any other organism known so far. They can neither generate nor store energy on their own. In fact, viruses depend on host cells for all their metabolic functions. What viruses can do, however, is infect, or cause disease.

Viruses are very different from bacteria, one of the minute microorganisms which can also cause disease. The most important difference between them is that bacteria are life forms having their own cells, and can be killed off by antibiotics, which cure disease infected by them by destroying their cell's metabolism. Viruses, however, use the host cell's metabolism, so antibiotics cannot affect them. If used, it will destroy the host cell.

But the startling discovery came during the period of World War I when scientists Frederick W. Twort and Felix. H Herelic in their independent studies found that even bacteria have been infected by an agent, now known to be viruses. They named it bacteriophage, 'eater of bacteria'. It meant that viruses are smaller than bacteria and can penetrate them too. So, viruses are small enough to be visible even through a simple microscope. They are almost invisible. But on the other side, it opened the doors for the study of viruses and how do they infect the host cell.

During those same years, people in Europe and America began to come down with a strange sleeping sickness, which became known as Encephalitis Lethargica. Victims would go to sleep and not wake up. They could be roused with great difficulty. However, the moment they were permitted to rest, they would at once sink back into deepest slumber and remain in that state for as long as they were left. Some went on in this manner for months before dying.

In 10 years, the disease killed some 5 million people then quietly went away. But the disease that had the whole world in its clutches was influenza. It first appeared in Boston in late August 1918. It killed 21 million people in the first four months. No one knows the global toll, as records in the third world were often poor, but it was not less than 20 million, probably as high as a hundred million.

This forced the investigators to devise a vaccine. In 1933 Wilson Smith, Christopher H Andrews, and Patrick P Laidlaw were able to transmit influenza to ferrets, and the influenza virus was adapted to mice.

In 1941 the American scientist George K Hirst found that the influenza virus grown in tissues of the chicken embryo could be detected by its capacity to draw together red blood cells. But for complete study viruses had to be dissected first.

In 1943 the electron microscope was developed. While the optical microscopes produced magnifications up to about 2000, electron microscopes produced magnifications of as much as 2 million. This permitted individual virus particles to be seen for the first time, leading to the classification of the virus and giving insight into their structure. Similarly, X-ray diffraction provided the basic structure of minute viruses.

Viruses occupy a special taxonomic position. All the viruses contain nucleic acid – either DNA or RNA- and protein. They form a shell called a capsid. Some viruses have an additional enclosure around the capsid called an envelope. The infective, extracellular form of a virus is called the virion. It contains at least one unique protein. Virions are disease-causing organisms that contain only nucleic acid and have no structural proteins. Other viruses like particles called prions are composed primarily of protein tightly packed within a small nucleic acid molecule. Prions can cause degenerative brain disease. Animal viruses exhibit extreme variation in size and shape. The smallest measure about 20nm in diameter. They contain nucleic acid with limited genetic information. In viruses, however, genetic information can come in single-stranded or double-stranded DNA or RNA, but not both.

"A virus is a strange and unlovely entity, a piece of nucleic acid surrounded by bad news" is a memorable phrase by 'Father of transplantation', Peter Medawar who won Nobel prize in 1960 for his work on immunology.

A significant advance was made by the American scientist John Enders, Thomas Weller, and Frederick Robbins who in 1949 developed the technique of cultivating cells on glass surfaces; cells could then be infected with the viruses to know how they invade and cause disease.

Applications of new knowledge about cell biology and biochemistry helped to determine how the invading viruses use nucleotides and amino acids of the host cell to synthesize its nucleic acids and proteins respectively. Some viruses use the lipids and sugar chains of the host cell. In many viruses, but not all, the nucleic acid alone, stripped of its capsid, can infect cells, although considerably less efficiently than can the intact virions. Certain viruses that cause serious diseases of animals and humans are carried by arthropods.

They concluded that viruses cannot replicate by themselves. They need to hijack host cells in order to replicate. A virus attaches itself to the target cell and then penetrates the cell wall of the host cell through either fusion with the cell membrane or translocation of the viral genetic material across the host cell membrane.

Once the host cell has been penetrated, the virus uses the cellular machinery of the host cell to replicate and make functional and structural viral proteins. The newly formed viral nucleic acid and structural proteins are then brought together to form the nucleocapsid of the virus. The newly formed viruses or virions are then released through a process called cell lysis which leads to the bursting of the host cell to release the virions. This also leads to the death of the host cell.

The cycle of infection occurring in seven stages often results in the death of the host cell and the release of many virus progenies. Certain viruses are called temperate or latent because the infection does not immediately result in cell death unless encountered by some factors or activated by certain other foreign elements.

Viruses that cause acute disease are generally, but not always, those that rapidly harm, or destroy cells, and have the capacity to shut off protein, or nucleic acid synthesis within the host cell. Most animal viruses penetrate cells in an intact form by a process called endocytosis.

Many viruses transmitted by the respiratory route (from sneezes and coughs) and limited to humans begin their cycle of infection in the upper respiratory tract (nose and throat) and then enter the bloodstream, where they are spread to distant tissues. How ill a person can get from the disease or how infectious the person may be, depends upon viral load. It refers to the amount of virus in the body of an infected person. A higher viral load at the time of symptom onset can mean that the virus can be transmitted easily.

Acute viral infections are of two types – local and systemic. Acute respiratory infections include the common cold and influenza. In the common cold, the virus infects only the nasal mucosa, while in influenza, the virus is found in both the nasal and bronchial mucosa, where damage can result in death. Other infections are flu-like illness localized in lymphoid tissue of the throat (although infection can occur in the intestine and the eye, or be spread to the heart), and severe respiratory infections of infants and children, which may be life-threatening.

Viruses have a bad reputation. Most of them cause serious, untreatable infections. It is very, very difficult to kill a virus because they are tough little critters. Even if their host dies, they lie dormant, waiting for an opportunity to infect another host and carry on the viral cycle. They have been known to lie dormant for thousands of years without losing potency.

Fortunately, the immune system of most animal species can fend off infection from many kinds of viruses. Every human being has in his or her cells the genes of viruses that lodged themselves in the genotype of our ancestors many millions of years ago. Altogether they make up 8%. More virus genes are being added all the time since some of the viruses that we are infected with during our lives also go on to integrate their DNA into our cells.

Some of the viruses are helpful, like the bacteriophage that lie in the soft tissues in the throats and noses of human beings. They target nasty bacteria that tend to proliferate in mucus. So, by preying on the bacteria that could cause mucus related infections, these viruses actually form a shield or a backup immune system for the hosts. Often, these infections do not cause any adverse effect at first, unless reactivated by stress.

Viruses possibly evolved from cells rather than cells from viruses. It seems likely that all viruses trace their origin to cellular genes and can be considered as pieces of rogue nucleic acids. Other possible progenitors of viruses are the plasmids, which can be transmitted.

That such agents have the ability to transmit efficiently from humans to humans was known to Kipchak Khan Janibeg in 1347, while he was besieging the Genoese trading port of Kafla in Crimea. Known as the Black Death, it decimated his army. With his forces disintegrating, Janibeg catapulted plague-infested corpses into the town in an effort to infect his enemies. Even the great and powerful, who were more capable to resist it, were struck down.

Who can forget the victory campaign of Alexander the Great? His invincible army refused to cross the Indus River because the soldiers were sick with flu and wanted to return home, despite much persuasions by Alexander. Alexander himself, only at the age of 33, died of viral fever in Babylon. Joan, daughter of the English King, Edward III, died while going to be wedded due to a viral infection.

Bird flu viruses have not yet acquired the ability to transmit efficiently from humans to humans, and are not known what genetic changes must take place for them to do so. But animal viruses are not only infectious but most of them mutate successfully and recur once again. From time to time certain strains of virus return. A disagreeable Russian virus known as H1N1 caused severe outbreaks over a wide area in 1933, then again in the 1950s, and yet again in the 1970s. Where it went in the meantime each time is uncertain. So is the case with influenza. The mystery behind this influenza virus was how it erupted suddenly all over the world.

First of all, Italy saw an outbreak of severe respiratory ailment in 1743. The English minister to Tuscany, Sir Horace Mann, wrote of Rome that 'Everybody is ill of influenza, and many die'. The epidemic spread throughout Europe. Italian influenza means 'influence' and derives from Latin fluere 'to flow'. The Italian word also had the sense 'an outbreak of an epidemic', so 'an epidemic'. Because of virus mutations that produce minor antigenic shifts about every 10 years, influenza viruses can resist inactivation by antibodies acquired by previous infection or vaccination. So, every mutation required a new counterattack, meaning thereby a new experiment.

In an attempt to devise a vaccine, medical authorities conducted experiments on volunteers at a military prison on Deer Island in Boston Harbour. The prisoners were promised a pardon if they survived a battery of tests. These tests were very rigorous, to say the least.

First, the subjects were injected with infected lung tissue taken from the dead and then spread in the eyes, nose, and mouth with infectious aerosols. If they still failed to succumb, they had their throats swabbed with discharges taken straight from the sick and dying. If all else failed, they were required to sit open-mouthed while a gravely ill victim was sat up slightly and made to cough into their faces.

Out of somewhat amazingly 300 men who volunteered, the doctors choose 62 for the tests. None contracted the flu, except the doctor, who was in charge of the experiment, and he died swiftly. The probable explanation for this is that the epidemic had passed through the prison a few weeks earlier and the volunteers, all of whom had survived the visitation, had natural immunity.

Vaccines are most successful when directed against those viruses that do not mutate and that infect only humans. Till date the only successful vaccine programme that has been carried out is polio. Polio viruses exist in only three antigenic types, each of which has not changed. They can prevent diseases caused by strictly human viruses that exist in only one antigenic and stable type. It is difficult to identify chemical compounds that inhibit the multiplication of viruses, but do not show the functions of, or are not toxic to the host cell. Certain natural products of cells, called interferons, may have potential antiviral and anticancer properties. Interferons are proteins normally synthesized by the cells of vertebrates, including humans.

Until recently, interferons were difficult to produce commercially because cells and tissues synthesize only small amounts of them. Through recombinant technology, however, large amounts of interferon can be produced. Although, its injections of large amounts can be harmful.

Like any other organism, viruses can be of different structures. They have six families to belong to. Coronovirdae is one of them. Viruses of this family have enveloped virions 120nm in diameter with a helical nucleocapsid containing a single strand of positive-sense RNA. Club-shaped glycoprotein gives it a crown-like (coronal) appearance. Viruses of this family are important agents of gastrointestinal disease in humans, poultry, and bovines. Any virus belonging to this family is known as coronavirus having enveloped virions. This is an animal virus.

In humans, a species known as SARS coronavirus causes a highly contagious disease. The virus emerged in humans in 2002; it likely jumped to humans from an animal reservoir, believed to be horseshoe bats. The ability of SARS coronavirus to jump to humans undoubtedly required genetic changes in the virus. These changes are suspected to have occurred in the civet. In 2012 another coronavirus capable of causing a severe respiratory illness later known as MERS was discovered in humans. Camels were identified as one possible reservoir for the MERS virus because it first appeared in Middle-east Asia.

Then in late 2019, in Wuhan, China, a patient with pneumonia of unknown cause was admitted to a local hospital. In the following weeks, the number of people with the same shortness of breath grew rapidly in Wuhan, and the disease spread to other regions of China. WHO identified it as COVID-19 and declared it a pandemic on March 11 the following year. Until then it had bedevilled to be spread in more than 110 countries of the world, officially infecting more than 118000 persons, and killing more than 4000. Naturally, many infections and deaths went unreported.

The virus does not linger in the air at high enough levels to be at risk to people. This virus can live for 3 days on some surfaces, like plastic and steel. But the research says the risk of consumers getting infected from touching those materials is still low. As we know, it takes seven steps for any virus to complete the cycle of infection. So, the symptoms showing infection take from 5-6 days to 14 days to appear. In most cases, it was found to be of 28 days. And symptoms start with dry cough and fever, which is generally ignored, resulting in loss of smell and/or taste. So, the probable answer to the pandemic effect of the virus is that it was incubated and spread by people who had only slight symptoms or none at all despite that they were carriers. And because they remained in circulation (movement), they would have spread the disease through their contacts.

Wuhan, the educational and research hub of China, was thought to be the eye of the storm, which swerved in all directions. But news from France rattled the scientific community when it was detected that the outbreak there was caused by a locally circulating strain of this virus.

Whenever WHO declares any disease pandemic, it consists of six phases of pandemic alert.

Phase I:- The lowest level of pandemic alert indicates that a virus either newly emerged or previously existing is circulating among animals. The risk of transmission to humans is low.

Phase II:- Isolated incidences of animal-to-human transmissions of the virus are observed indicating that the virus has pandemic potential.

Phase III:- When it turns into multiple cases, though the limited capacity for human-to-human transmission may be present.

Phase IV:- Confirmed human-to-human viral transmission that causes sustained disease in human communities. At this stage, containment of the virus is deemed impossible, but a pandemic is not necessarily inevitable. The implementation of control methods is the emphasis on not to spread it further.

Phase V:- Marked by human-to-human disease transmission in two countries, indicating that a pandemic is imminent and that distribution of stockpiled drugs and execution of strategies to control the disease must be carried out with a sense of urgency.

Phase VI:- It is the highest level. It is characterized by widespread and sustained disease transmission among humans.

The present pandemic caused by coronavirus is identified to be in the sixth phase, which calls for greater attention. It has the same effect as the greatest epidemic influenza had.

Researchers note that the viral load profile of SARS COV-2 is similar to that of influenza. It peaks at around the time of symptom onset. A higher viral load at the time of symptom onset can mean that the virus can be transmitted easily, even when the symptoms are relatively mild. The same characteristic of influenza made it the worst ever epidemic in the history of mankind. In a host animal or cell culture, the seven-step process is repeated many times, the progeny virions released from the original site of infection are then transmitted to other sites or to the individuals. So frequent hand-washing, masking the face, and social distancing are stressed upon.

At the moment, there is no cure for infection with the coronavirus behind the COVID-19. However, different types of drugs, methodologies, and injections are being tested on human patients for their ability to fight off infection or to reduce the severity of the disease, but to no avail.

Dexamethasone, a steroid, has reduced death rates in COVID-19 patients who need to be put on ventilation or are given oxygen support. However, this line of treatment is for those whose condition is severe enough and can actually harm patients if given too soon, as it could hamper a helpful immune response.

Out of several methods, plasma therapy is also used. Plasma is derived when all the blood cells are separated from whole blood, and what is left, is 90% water. But it contains critical solutes necessary for the treatment if it has already been injected with antiviral drugs used for their cure from the said disease. It also has sporadic results. Many antiviral drugs were tested like Remdesivir (it can work against viruses that have already entered cells), but as we already know every virus has its own cure.

Drugs or vaccines invented by Blumberg against Hepatitis B, which won him a Nobel prize, cannot be effective against coronavirus. For this, fresh research like Blumberg is required.

The 2020 Nobel Prize for medicine that was awarded jointly to American researchers Harvey Alter, Charles Rice, and British scientist Michael Houghton for their work in identifying the Hepatitis C virus is proof of it. They had devoted decades to work that helped to limit the spread of the fatal disease and developed antiviral drugs to cure it. The drugs used to cure liver diseases caused by Hepatitis B couldn't cure the same diseases spread by blood transfusions.

Baruch S. Blumberg, an American research physician whose discovery of an antigen that provokes antibody response against Hepatitis B led to the development by the other researchers of a successful vaccine against the disease. Such an antibody protects against further infection.

The challenge in vaccine development consists of devising a vaccine strong enough to ward off infection without making the individual seriously ill. Vaccines may consist of coronaviruses that have lost the ability to cause serious illness but retain the ability to stimulate immunity or may contain viruses that have been killed or inactivated with heat or chemicals. It may be a subunit vaccine, which is made from proteins found on the surface of the virus.

Medical researchers are trying to identify the genes of a pathogen that encode the protein or proteins that stimulate the immune response to the virus. This will allow the immunity-stimulating proteins (called antigens) to be mass-produced and used in the vaccine.

Unless and until that type of antibody is developed, there is no permanent solution. It means proper antigen is required for this antimen microorganism. The possibility that the virus can revisit us is very high, as happened in China.

Moreover, most of us are anonymous carriers. A research paper in Britain has indicated that with such an impact of coronavirus on human lives and no major achievement in the development of drugs and vaccines to counter it, total elimination of this virus would not be possible before 2024. And it is true for all viruses.

The virus that caused the 1957 pandemic which lasted until about the middle of 1958 was also responsible for a series of epidemics that emerged annually until 1968 when the Hongkong flu appeared. The present virus has the same damaging effect to recur again and again.

According to 'official' figures in the world, over 213 countries and territories had reported 30,353,736 confirmed cases of COVID-19, and a death toll of 961,403 patients within 6 months of its being declared a pandemic by WHO. Most of the cases went unreported. The head of emergencies at the WHO roughly confirms this. According to him its 'best practices' indicate that roughly 1 in 10 people worldwide have been infected by the coronavirus. The estimate which would amount to over 760 million people based on the current world population of about 7.6 billion far outstrips the number of confirmed cases. In fact, the number of cases greatly underestimates the true figure.

The U.S topped the list with 6,713,179 cases and a death toll crossing 203,824. The data are quite surprising. The U.S that has given the world a total of 336 Noble laureates, many of whom belonged to the field of physiology, having a density of only 92.9 residents per square mile, and boasting a literacy rate of almost 100% has been so worst affected. The mighty nation, with 2062 active satellites in space, most of which are spy satellites, couldn't locate the deaths happening due to virus in China and warn the world accordingly.

The recommended test till date is RT-PCR. It identifies a CT value for each sample that has been tested. CT value indicates the number of cycles needed in the RT-PCR test to amplify viral RNA, so it can reach a detectable level. A lower CT value is a sign of high viral load. If CT (threshold cycle) value is above 45, it will be considered Negative. If it is between 40 and 45, it is marginally positive. A CT value of 38-40 indicates minimal viral load, while 30-37 moderate. A lower CT value, 29 or below, is a sign of high viral load.

Now scientists have developed a new simplified Covid-19 diagnostic test which is an RBD-based antibody test. Receptor binding domain or RBD is the unique protein on the virus that enables the virus to gain entry into host cells. The test can measure the levels of this protein, which they said correlates to the levels of the body's neutralizing antibodies that provide immunity in infected individuals.

The high and mighty, who were found positive, were U.S President Donald Trump and First Lady Melania Trump, American singer Madonna, Indian matinee idol Amitabh Bachhan, Russian PM Mikhail Mishtusin, British PM Boris

Johnson, Prince Charles, wife of Canadian PM, Israeli health minister, British health minister, and Iran deputy health minister. The entire world was under lockdown continuously for 3 to 4 months to avoid community spread.

The most important coronal effect that was seen during this lockdown world over was that for the first time humans were caged, and through the windows of their cages, they saw wild animals roaming freely without any fear of being attacked and killed. The air quality level suddenly improved due to less pollution. The living style of humankind subtracted.

This invisible antimen has reduced the definition of Aristotle from "Man is a social animal" to "Man is a social-site animal".

Estado da India

In the 16th and 17th centuries, global economic power was largely concentrated in Asian empires – Ottoman Turkey, Safavid Persia, Mughal Hindustan, Ming, and then Qing China – who controlled the diverse trade networks linking them to the Spice Islands, Africa, Arabia, and Europe.

Many European nations were eyeing towards this lucrative trade. India at that time was one of their main targets. The sea route via the Cape of Good Hope was the major artery which later sustained European colonial supremacy in the subcontinent. It was an India in which the chief powers were still Asian rather than European.

The Hindu ruled kingdom of Vijaynagar, abutted by the Malabar kingdoms of Calicut, Cannanore, and Quilon was the principal power in the south until a military defeat by the Deccan Sultanates in 1565 prompted its eventual demise in 1646. The Portuguese militarized the East African coast and the Arabian Sea in the 16th century, wresting control of the old maritime trade routes from the Arabs, the Persians, and other local merchants. This allowed them to gain footholds in Goa and parts of the Malabar coast, including Cochin; they also acquired Daman and Diu from the Sultan of Gujarat.

When Albuquerque finally captured Goa, killed all the Muslims, and appointed a Hindu, Timoja, 'Governor of Goa',

Goa was the first territorial possession of the Portuguese in Asia. Goa became the capital of the whole Portuguese empire in Asia. It was their Estado da India. It was granted the same civic privileges as in Lisbon, reaching the climax of its prosperity between 1575 and 1600. Even the British didn't dare to make their presence felt there, except for a short period.

Portuguese Government opened the application counter for home country passports. Portuguese passports acquired greater allure after the country became a member of the European Union in 1986, which now allows un-fettered movement and employment across 28 countries, it also allows visa-free travel across more than 170 countries. Portuguese citizenship proved to be a shortcut to reach Britain. Anyone can apply for Portuguese citizenship on the basis of their birth during the period of Portuguese sovereignty.

African Facts

Africa is the second largest continent after Asia. About half of the population is under 15 years old. Africa has many resources, but they are unevenly distributed. Libya and Nigeria are leading oil producers, Southern Africa is rich in gold and diamonds, and Zambia is a leading copper producer. Kenya leads the world in the export of pyrethrum, a pink flower that is dried to make insecticides. With its young population and resources, Africa is poised to play an important economic role in the future and hence its markets and resources are being eyed by major countries including India and China. Africa also has many strange facts, unknown to us before.

Civilization in Africa began to appear more than 5000 years ago with the rise of ancient Egypt. From about 2500 years ago in sub-Saharan Africa, many other different kingdoms also developed. The Sahara acted as a barrier to keep this area separate from the rest of the world until the arrival of Arab traders in the 8th century. About 40% of Africa is desert like the erg of Bilma in Niger which is a part of the vast Sahara. In Arabic, erg means a sandy expanse. The Sahara was once a fertile land rich in plants and animals. But thousands of years ago, it dried up, and people moved south to the Savannah to farm there. Undaunted by this fact, the Great Man-made project was set up to irrigate farming land.

Water is piped from beneath the Sahara to populated coastal regions.

Not only desert, but Africa has also one of the longest rivers in the world, the Congo formerly Zaire, which flows in a great curve crossing the equator twice. Not to be left behind in the field of education, Kaureein University, founded in Fes in Morocco, in AD 859, is the oldest in the world. No other continent matches the wealth of wildlife found in Africa. Known for its elephants, it is home to many birds. Sandgrouse is one of them. Despite living in the open desert, Sandgrouse must drink regularly. This often means flying long distances. Sandgrouse obtains water for their young by immersing themselves in water and carrying droplets back to their nests in their feathers.

And most importantly, Niger, a country in Africa is famous for the male beauty contest. Every year, in a festival known as Gerewol, young Wodabbe men make themselves up to try and attract a wife in an unusual beauty contest. After much dancing, women make their choice. If a marriage proposal results, the man kidnaps the woman, and they set off into the desert for a nomadic life together.

Lakshmi Vandana

Lakshmi, meaning "Prosperity", the daughter of Bhrigu, the bride of Vishnu, represents the social order and settled married life. She is described in texts as beautifully dressed and decked with ornaments.

According to the Puranas, she was the daughter of Bhrigu and Khyati. It was at a subsequent period that she was produced from the sea at the churning of the ocean. She is the bride of Vishnu. When Hari was born as a dwarf, Lakshmi appeared from lotus (as Padma or Kamala). When he was born as the Rama of the race of Bhrigu as Parshuram, she was Dharani. When he was Raghava (Ram Chandra), she was Sita. And when he was Krishna she became Rukmini. The Tattriya Sanhita makes Lakshmi and Sri to be two wives of Aditya, and the Satpatha Brahmana describes Sri as issuing forth from Prajapati.

She is also the daughter of the milky sea as having been born from the churning of the ocean. She has been compared to Aphrodite in Greek mythology. Aphrodite was born from the white foam produced by the severed genitals of Uranus (Heaven), after his son, Cronus threw them into the sea. The Greek word aphros means "foam". She was, like Lakshmi, known primarily as a goddess of love and fertility and even occasionally presided over marriage.

Lakshmi was praised in Ramayana as "Kshirbhi-Tanya", which has been translated into English by Ralph T.H. Griffith as such:

At length when many a year had fled,

Up floated, on her lotus bed,

A maiden fair and tender-eyed,

In the young flush of beauty's pride.

She shone with pearl and golden sheen,

And seals of glory stamped her queen.

On each round arm glowed many a gem,

On her smooth brows, a diadem.

Rolling in waves beneath her crown

The glory of her hair flowed down.

Pearls on her neck of price untold,

The lady shone like burnished gold.

Queen of the Gods, she leapt to land,

A lotus in her perfect hand,

And fondly, of the lotus sprung,

To lotus-bearing, Vishnu clung.

Her, Gods above and men below

As beauty's queen and Fortune know.

Yum Hain Hum

This was the name of a popular TV serial on Indian Television. The show was based on the theme of a divine solution to human problems and the interactions between divinity and humanity. The divine solution is provided by Yumraj – the God of death, and his aide Chitragupta as they descend on the earth to get the first-hand experience of what the humans think about them. In fact, humans are surprised to find them in a much simpler form, quite opposite to what they knew about them. What would humans see when they visit Yumloka, the abode of the dead, instead?

According to the Hindu texts, Yumaraj was the first of mortals who died, and discovered the way to the other world; he guides other men thither and assembles them in a home which is secured to them forever. He is the monarch of the Pitris and judge of the dead. He is a king and dwells in celestial light. He lives in Pitriloka with his four wives namely Dhumrorna, Hemamala, Sushila, and Vijaya, in his city of Yumapuri, where he has a huge palace called Kalichi.

He is of green colour and has four arms. Seated on a buffalo, his consort Dhumrorana sits on his left lap. His right hands hold staff and a sword, while his left hands have a trident with flames and a mala or rosary. He sits upon his throne of judgement Vichara-bhu. His two custodians are Maha-Chanda and Kalapurusha. The door of his judgement hall is kept by his porter – Vaidhyata.

To his right stands Chitragupta, his chief attendant in northern dress (Udichyavesna) and Kalapurusha holding a noose, which he tightens around his victims. Chitragupta has 32 arms, as big as three yojanas. His red eyes resemble oblong ponds.

Yumaraj has also two insatiable dogs, with four eyes and wide nostrils known as Sarameyas which guard the road to his abode, and which the departed are advised to hurry past with all possible speed. These dogs wander among men as Yumaraj's messengers, to summon men to the presence of their master, who is in another place identified with death.

His chief assistant Chitragupta who has recorded the deeds of each person in a huge register called Agrasandhani tells his master all about the victim. Yama judges the dead and assigns them to different regions. According to its deeds, the soul is sent to the world of the Pitris, or is reborn, or is sent to one of 28 hells or Narakas. And the following message is forwarded to the earth:

The good which thou on earth has wrought,

Each sacrifice, each pious deed,

Shall there receive its ample meed;

No worthy act shall be forgot.

The Jewel Power

There is a dispute over the ownership of the Koh-i-Noor diamond between India and England.

The 107-carat stone, Koh-i-Noor meaning "mountain of light" was once the largest cut diamond in the world. Believed to have been mined in India nearly 800 years ago, it most likely formed part of the loot of Nadir Shah in 1739. After his death, it fell into the hands of his General, Ahmad Shah, founder of the Durrani dynasty of Afghan. His descendant, Shah Shuja, when a fugitive in India, was forced to surrender it to Ranjit Singh. The Marquess of Dalhousie, the British governor-general arranged for it to be presented to Queen Victoria after the British colonization of Punjab in 1849. The last Sikh ruler, Duleep Singh, a 13-year-old boy was made to travel to Britain in 1850 when he handed the gem to Queen Victoria. The Koh-i-Noor remains part of the crown fashioned for use by Queen VI, Elizabeth, consort of George VI, since then.

The famous diamond was once a part of Takht-i-Tavus, the legendary peacock throne of Shahjahan. Shahjahan had specially ordered it for making of this throne before he left Agra for the Deccan in 1630. It took 2 years to complete the project. He had demanded 'that two hundred times a hundred thousand livres should be spent on his throne in gold, diamonds, rubies, pearls, and emeralds'. Such was the inkling of the Mughal emperors for the precious stones. The French traveller, Jean-Baptiste Tavernier, devotes an extended sequence of his "Travels in India" to describing the precious stones he was shown in Agra by the Mughal treasurer Akil Khan including the famed Koh-i-Noor diamond.

A similar throne was ordered for Jehangir in 1616 which took 3 years to complete. It was presented to the emperor as part of the lavish Navroz celebrations organized by his Prime Minister, Itmad-ud-Daulah in March 1619, which Jehangir used to sit once a year only for nine days. This throne was supported by four lions weighing 150 quintals of silver covered with beaten gold leaf, and the canopy was supported by 12 columns in which there were 12,000 ounces of enamelled gold. Jehangir himself estimated its cost at an astonishing 450,000 rupees. Noor Jehan's treasure was itself a witness to the many functions of a well-cut jewel.

The thread leads us to the great Mughal Emperor Akbar, who not had only a strong predilection for the precious stones but also a penchant for international jewellery. Akbar had dubbed nine exceptionally talented courtiers his Navratnas. The mosques, that were built inside the Agra fort, was named Nagina Masjid and Moti Masjid. Agra fort is itself a display case for another Mughal art form; exquisitely designed jewellery. Upon Akbar's death in 1605, according to a Flemish visitor's calculations, his 'diamonds, rubies, emeralds, sapphires, pearls, and similar jewels' would have a value of '60,520,521 rupees'.

The Sword over Tipu Sultan

Every year conflicts arise between proponents and opponents over the celebration of Tipu's birth anniversary in the month of November. Some consider him nationalist while some do not.

There is much confusion about Tipu's role in Indian history. Tipu's legacy has always been a matter of debate among historians.

Tipu was the Sultan of Mysore from 1783 to 1798. Mysore was the capital of the Wodeyar rulers, who were governors of southern Karnataka under the Vijayanagar kings. The Wodeyar dynasty ruled almost uninterrupted from 1399 until Independence, except for the 38-years ruled by the Muslim warlord Haider Ali and his son Tipu Sultan.

Haider Ali, an adventurer, as well as his son and successor Tipu Sultan, were by temperament domineering, but with skillful tolerance they made the people forget that they had displaced the traditional dynasty. It is said that the people were happy under their rule. In their external policies, they showed rare farsightedness. Haider Ali was more forthcoming in this sense. Haider Ali had turned Mysore's forces into a professional army, trained, equipped, and paid along European lines. Tipu was determined sincerely to modernize his economy.

Tipu Sultan had his father's ferocity but none of his wisdom, alternating between sadistic foppery and bouts of Muslim fanaticism, was constant only in his wish to get rid of the English. During this time, the Anglo-French rivalry was at its peak. That foreigners became involved in the internal conflicts was an unavoidable consequence of the disunity of India.

India became a theatre of war for European conflicts. It was shameful that the European powers should fight such wars with Indian mercenaries and often with Indian money. The enemy of the enemy is a friend. The theory worked for both Tipu Sultan and the French who lovingly called him Tipoo. But Tipu did not have that luck. When Tipu Sultan asked for French help, a French Fleet under Admiral Suffren appeared from Mauritius, which was at that time headquarter of the French Fleet in the Indian Ocean but was withdrawn after the Treaty of Versailles which put an end to the war between France and England, compelling Tipu to carry the war alone.

For some time more Tipu carried on the war single-handed against Governor-General Wellesley, but he was overpowered at the battle of Srirangapatnam, where he died a true soldier's death. Tipu Sultan had even vented his frustration at his inability to defeat the British by ordering a special life-size toy, replete with the sound of a tiger killing a British soldier. A vindictive and sometimes cruel autocrat he readily antagonized his enemies, both Indian and British, and was easily demonized by them.

With this, died his dream of associating with Napolean in his fight against the British. When Napoleon landed in Egypt, obviously his first step was towards intervention in India, but it was too late for Tipoo. With that, the resistance of the Moslem successor states came to an end. Amongst the Moslem rulers, Haider and Tipu fought till last, but they represented neither a state nor people. Basically, they were adventurers who had nothing to lose but their lives.

Despite all this, there should be no dispute over the events of history. Had the disputants been witness to those Anglo-Mysore wars, whom would have they supported? In fact, India had only been the witness of wars between foreign elements being fought at its land and at its cost.

Leap of Faith

Sikhs display their martial skills in the processions as part of the celebration of Guru Nanak's Jayanti. But that was not intended to be when Guru Nanak founded this religion. As a child, he had been in touch with both Hindu Pandit and Muslim Maulavi. But in 1496 he had a mystical experience, when he went into the Bein river to bathe, and disappeared.

All had given him up for dead, but he reappeared after 3 days, and the first words he is reported to have said are: "There is no Hindu or no Mussalman". The essence of the teachings, he was soon to reveal, was received by him in a divine vision. He was always accompanied by his two disciples, Mardana-a Muslim, and Bala-a Hindu.

Originally the followers of Guru Nanak were known as Shishyas, which later became Sikhs. After Guru Nanak, three Gurus followed and expanded his principles. After the fifth Guru, Arjan Dev was executed by the Mughal Emperor Jehangir in 1606, the nature of the Sikh community began to change, and Sikhs began to organize themselves as a military force.

This process intensified after the martyrdom of Guru Tegh Bahadur in 1675. Guru Gobind Singh, the tenth Guru founded the Khalsa and promoted the concept of the santsipahi. According to the Rahit Maryada, a guide to Sikhism, "A Sikh is any man or woman who believes in one God, in the 10 Gurus, who has the faith in the Amrit of the tenth Guru and who professes no other religion". Amrit refers to the Khalsa ceremony.

His Master's Voice

Ustad Sabri Khan, the Sarangi maestro, is credited for giving Sarangi a new lease of life. He had played Vande Matram that rang through the Parliament a minute past midnight as India ushered in Independence. He was the musician who was brought to Nehru's sickbed in his last days in an effort to soothe him with his melody. Naturally, he was one of the favourites of Nehru.

Tansen was also one of the Navratnas in Akbar's court. It is said that when he sang one of the Night Rags at mid-day; it immediately became night and the darkness extended in a circle round the palace as far as his voice could be heard.

But there was also an unsung musician in the reign of Akbar – Naik Gopal. One day he was commanded by the emperor to sing the Rag Deepak, which whoever attempted to sing should be destroyed by the fire. Naik Gopal flew to the river Yamuna and plunged himself up to the neck in water, but Akbar, determined to prove the power of this rag, compelled the unfortunate musician to sing it. Notwithstanding his situation in the river, flames burst violently from his body and consumed him to ashes.

The Happiness Factor

A study published in The Lancet finds that the widely held view that happiness enhances health and longevity is unfounded. The new study says earlier research confused cause and effect, suggesting that unhappiness made people ill when it is actually the other way around. But it also warned that unhappiness itself may not affect health directly, it can do harm emotionally. Happiness is a squishy measure.

Being happy is a process, not an event. It is a journey, not a destination. It is not where you arrive, it is how you get here. Happiness is living in a way that brings peace and contentment into our life regardless of the circumstances. It is not only our right but in a way our responsibility to be happy.

In the *Idiot* by way of the hero, Dostoevsky tries to establish that happiness is a matter of the very process of living. Columbus, he explains, was happy not when he discovered America but while he was discovering it.

Let us make a set of principles to stay happy, and name it P-E-A-S-E-F-U-L.

Where P is for Perception: How we see the world and how we see others is a significant determinant of our happiness.

E is for Emotional Generosity: It means that you give other human beings the benefit of the doubt.

A is for Acceptance and Abundance: Acceptance is a way to get past denial and into action. Abundance is a mindset that there is plenty for everyone.

S is for Surrender: It is giving up on results, no longer prescribing the outcome, and letting go of control and manipulation.

E is for Empowering Yourself and Others: Doing all we can with love, compassion, and kindness empowers us to be happy and in turn those around us to be happy as well.

F is for Forgiveness: Every offence that has occurred in the past only has life as long as it lives in our memory.

U is for Underreact: Choosing to underreact is choosing peace and love over anything else.

L is for Love: Any action or response is either love or a cry for love. It brings with it the power to dissolve all negativity and conflict.

So, no matter what, we can always remain happy.

The Sick Samrat

Delhi's air quality has always been a concern. Everyone is of the opinion that it has been due to emissions from the vehicles, which have almost clogged Delhi's roads. Although the corona effect had improved it, but it is now back to square one. It raises the question, "Was Delhi safe in historical times?"

Since history books do not mention pollution at that time, it is very difficult to find its answer. Delhi became a part of regular history since Shahjahan built Shahjahanabad which is now old Delhi. It was a fashion of that time for Samrats and lords to keep personal physicians, who were foreigners because they didn't believe Indian medical practices. Francois Bernier was one of such physicians. He was a French Doctor who journeyed to Delhi in the 1660s and served a Mughal lord, Danishmand Khan. After his period of service with Danishmand Khan, Bernier subsequently became a personal physician to the Mughal Emperor Aurangzeb. He has recorded this period in his book "Travels in the Mughal India".

In this book, he writes about a travel with the Mughal court to Kashmir. The journey was undertaken for medical reasons; Aurangzeb had suffered from a spell of illness and was convinced that relocation to a safer climate would benefit his health 'by the change of air'.

According to Bernier, the entire population of Delhi, about 200000 humans, and 100000 animals accompanied Aurangzeb to ensure his protection. Although the causes of Aurangzeb's illness are unclear, Bernier welcomed the change. In his view, Delhi's environment was not conducive to the emperor's health. He also remarks of Delhi's drinking water that 'fevers most difficult to cure are engendered by it'. Aurangzeb had earlier suffered a paralysis of the tongue and very nearly lost his power of speech entirely.

Dostana

Aligarh is a 2015 Indian movie based on the real-life incident of Dr Shrinivas Ramchandra Siras. Dr Siras was the professor of Marathi at Aligarh Muslim University, who was suspended from his job because of his sexual orientation towards a rickshawala. After successfully appealing his suspension, he died in suspicious circumstances way back in 2010. After a long silence, the rickshawala revealed that he had also tried to end his life after the death of his true 'Saathi' but failed in his attempt. Such type of 'Dostana' has no borders.

One of such incidents relate to the period when cosmopolitanism was at its peak along the trading artery of the Silk Route when mingling of ideas was as much common as the exchange of commodities. The route also contributed to the spread of ghazal, the tightly structured, rhymed love poetry that expressed the exquisite pain of loss and separation. Transmitted partly by wandering Sufis and partly by travelling merchants across Central and South Asia, the ghazal's distinctive preoccupation with separation resonated in particular for people who had left their homes.

Sai'd Sarmad Koshani was one of the Jewish traders from Kashan in Central Asia. His business took him, in approximately 1632, to Thatta, near the Indus River in what is now the Pakistani Province of Sindh.

The river-city was at that point part of the Mughal Empire. It was also a Sufi cultural centre, and ghazal recitals were common there among not just its Muslim but also its Hindu inhabitants. It was here, one night, that Sarmad attended a Mushaira and heard the performance of a ghazal by a young teenage boy named Abhai Chand, a Hindu of the Vaishya caste.

The presentation captivated Sarmad in such a way that he fell head over heels in love with the boy, but this 'Dostana' required parents' approval. He worked on Abhai Chand's parents, who were initially horrified by Sarmad's interest in their son. The father hid the boy and alerted the authorities. Sarmad responded by taking off his clothes and sitting completely naked at the parents' doorstep for several days and nights.

Astonishingly, this seems to have convinced Abhai Chand's parents that Sarmad's love was pure. This 'Dostana' proved transformative for both Sarmad and Abhai Chand. In Sarmad's company the boy adapted the life of a mendicant beggar, Sarmad too was never the same. From the time he undressed outside Abhai Chand's house, he refused to wear clothes.

Alexander the Great's love for his male friend Hephaeston is also well known. It is reported that when Hephaeston died, Alexander was plagued by dreams of his own death.

The Willpower Trap

Every year we make new promises to ourselves and find most of them unfulfilled at the end of the year. As a result, we blame no one but ourselves for making the wrong choices. When people believe that their ability to make good choices stems from nothing more than their willpower and that willpower is a quality they're either born with or they're not – they eventually stop trying together. This is the willpower trap that keeps them in a depressing cycle, that begins with heroic commitment to change, which is followed by eroding motivation and terminated inevitably by relapsing into old ways.

"Where there is a will, there is a way" is an old say. It has to be strengthened by a new say "If change is taking too much will, it's probably because we lack skill".

When change seems hard, we blame our character, but our character is usually not to blame. We are blind to the crucial role skills play in creating and sustaining change. Many of the toughest challenges we face are difficult because they test our willpower. Will is a skill, not a character trait. Willpower can be learnt and strengthened like anything else, and it is best learnt through deliberate practice.

The City of Nectar

Madurai is known as "The City of Nectar". It was founded by Kulasekara. He was as strong as Pandi (Bull), so the foundation of the Pandyan Dynasty. He was a devout follower of Shiva. According to the legend, he once had a dream of Sundareshwara (as Shiva known in the South) requesting to make an abode for Him. The king devoutly followed the dream and thus completed the city. On the auspicious day of the city's consecration, Shiva himself appeared and showered the land with maduram (nectar) from the crescent Moon in his matted locks.

Thus, was born Madurai, the City of Nectar on the banks of the Vaigai river. The movement of the great Naga or serpent marked the boundaries of the city, and the famous Meenakshi Temple was built where its tail and head met. From the 7th to 13th centuries, as the capital of the Pandyas, it saw art and trade from Rome and China flourish. It later became a part of the Vijaynagar Empire and was the Nayaka capital in the 16th and 17th centuries. It was also a host to the famous Tamil Sangams which were to provide Tamil literature with some of its most enduring works.

Madurai is famous for its temples most notably for Meenakshi Temple. Meenakshi is another name of Parvati. According to the legend, she was the daughter of King

Malaydwaja of Madurai and Kanchanmala, daughter of the Chola King, Susenan. She was named that because the fish was once the emblem of the Pandyan dynasty.

Although beautiful, there was one anomaly in her appearance – she had three breasts. The king was upset with this deformity in her daughter. Just then a voice from the heavens proclaimed, "She is Thadaathagai – the Invincible One, endowed with dauntless valour. When she is to meet the one who is to wed her, her third breast will disappear". From then on, she dressed and acted like a boy, and after ascending the throne on her father's death, she went on a campaign to bring the whole world under her rule. Leading her army, she won battles everywhere, until she reached Mt Kailasha, the abode of Shiva. There she fell in love, her third breast disappeared, and she became Shiva's wife.

The entire city of Madurai is built around one grand structure called the Meenakshi Sundareshwara Temple. The temple is known as Meenakshi Temple, but it has all the 64 acts of Shiva as murals believed to have been performed in Madurai. It was originally built by the early Pandyas (7th – 10th centuries) but it was redesigned in the present form by Vishwanatha Nayala in 1560 during the reign of Thirumalai Nayak.

One of the important festivals of the temple is the Meenakshi Thirukalyanam, the divine marriage of Meenakshi (Parvati) and Sundareshwara (Shiva), which is celebrated as a part of Tamil New Year Chitrai (in April-May). The images of Sundareshwara and Meenakshi are decorated with jewels and pearl crowns and taken out in procession.

The God Alagar (Vishnu) then comes to give his sister Meenakshi in marriage to Sundareshwara. According to the legend associated with the marriage, he was late for the marriage and it took place without him because he was dallying with a princess in Alagar Koli, said to have been built by Vishwakarma for Vishnu on the insistence of Yama at the foot of the Alagar hills. He is depicted in various postures, seated, standing, and reclining. This incident is re-enacted every year whenever the festival takes place.

The Power of Virginity

Kanyakumari is the place where pilgrims gather to watch the sunset at the point where India ends and beyond which there is only water and no land. The most breathtaking of these occurs on Chaitra Purnima when both sunset and moonrise occur at the same time. It is the place where the Indian Ocean, the Arabian Sea, and the Bay of Bengal meet.

The place is named after a Hindu goddess who is worshipped without a male consort and a temple is dedicated to her namely Kumari Amman Temple. The processional deity in the temple is known as Tyagasundari while the deity ready for marriage is known as Syamasundari. She was named Pushpakashi. She loved the God Shiva and wished to marry him and meditated on Mt Kailasha for hundreds of years. Shiva knew she had great powers that he didn't want to destroy. So, she was granted the wish on the condition that she would have to go to the southernmost point, to vanquish the Asura Bana, and then to wait for him. She succeeded in her project, but Shiva insisted they wait until a later incarnation.

Believing that if she performed an arduous penance once again, she would attract the attention of her beloved, the goddess subjected herself to harsh austerities. The temple is located at the place where she undertook severe penance to obtain Lord Shiva's hand in marriage. It is believed that the sparkling nose-ring of the deity can be seen from the sea. Of the two rocks that lie to the southeast of the temple, one is said to bear the foot-prints (Sripadaparai) of the virgin goddess. Suchindram is the place where Shiva is said to have rested on the banks of the Palayar river, while the goddess performed her penance at Kanyakumari. And the marriage never took place, since it was deemed that she remain a virgin in order to save the world.

Authentic Indian

India is a diverse multi-ethnic country that is home to thousands of small and ethnic tribal groups. That complexity developed from a lengthy and involved process of migration and intermarriage.

Being geographically convenient to reach, India was repeatedly invaded by foreigners and migrants over the millennia. Although several races had entered India in one way or the other, in time they all had merged indistinguishably into the Indian social-cultural milieu till the Turkish invasion. India had absorbed all the pre-Turkish invaders and migrants into its society and culture because India was then, a marvellously vital and creative civilization.

India in pre-modern times was often regarded by foreigners as a paradise on earth. Through its northwest, it has added Mongolian, Afghan, Greek, Persian, Arab, Armenian, and Jewish DNA to India's exceptionally diverse genetic mix. As a result of migrations through the northeast, Chinese, Tibetan, Thai, and Burmese genes have also mingled with the local pool. And countless waves of maritime migrations have brought people from all over the world, from Yemen, Syrian, African, Australoid, and Europeans to the subcontinent. Keeping in view of this fact it is very difficult to tell who is authentically Indian.

In fact, all Indians ultimately have some foreign ancestry. Becoming Indian is intimately connected to a process of India-building. And in the process of becoming Indian, one must make India something better than what it is. As an early 14th century Persian writer states:

It is asserted that paradise is in India

Be not surprised because paradise itself is not comparable to it.

To prove our authenticity, let us make India paradise once again.

High-flying Balloons

A man was selling balloons on a busy street of a city. He knew how to attract a crowd before he offered his wares for sale. He took a white balloon, filled it up, and let it float upward. Next, he filled a red balloon and released it. Then he added a yellow one. As the red, white, and yellow balloons were floating above his head, the little children gathered around to buy his balloons.

A hesitant boy looked up at the balloons and finally asked, "if you filled a black balloon, would it go up too?"

The man looked down and said, "Why, sure! It's not the colour of the balloon, it's what's inside that makes it go up!"

Similarly, what's inside of us determines whether we achieve peak success experience in our life or not. Climbing to the peak depends upon our minds and our attitudes.

The Emotional Town

Rameshwaram is a sacred town situated on Pamban Island in the Gulf of Mannar, in the Laccadive sea of the Indian Ocean at the tip of the Indian Peninsula. It is referred to as "Varanasi of the South". It is connected to the mainland by a 1 km bridge, on the one side of which flows the Indian Ocean and on the other Bay of Bengal. It is also well-connected by rail to cities like Chennai, Madurai, and Trichy through a rail bridge over the Indian Ocean.

This is the place where Rama worshipped Shiva to seek his approbation after killing Ravana, who was Brahmana from the paternal side. He was the grandson of the Rishi Pulastya and the son of Visharwa by his wife Kaikasi or Nikasha, the daughter of the Rakshash Sumali. The island overlooks Gandhmandana hill that has a temple on it where the footprint of Lord Rama is enshrined. It has a temple named Ramanathaswamy temple that houses two Shivalingas.

According to the story attached to it, when Rama decided to worship his God to expiate the sin of killing a Brahman, he ordered Hanuman to bring a Shivalinga for the purpose. Hanuman as usual took the flight to bring the biggest one, but the search took its own time. When Sita saw Ram perturbed by the delay, as the auspicious time was nearing, she made a small Shivalinga from sand which finally Rama worshipped. It is enshrined in the main sanctuary as the linga of Sri Ramanatha. The installation ceremony of the linga by Sita is celebrated every year. The second which Hanuman brought is known as Vishwalinga or the linga of Vishwanatha.

Apart from these two shrines, there are others dedicated to Vishalakshi, consort of Vishwanatha, Parvati, consort of Ramanatha, and Vishnu, known here as Setumadhava. The visit to the main Shivalinga is an adventure in itself. According to the tradition followed in this temple, the devotees have first to take a dip into the Indian Ocean and then the attendants pour water over them from 22 Tirthas (sacred wells), which is said to have curative value also. The way from one Tirtha to the 22nd Tirtha is in the structure of ohm.

Rameshwaram is also famous for having one of the 12 Jyotirlingas. It has a unique structure spanning across the ocean, which is mentioned in both Hindu and Christian mythology. It teaches us that if you have the courage, determination, and strong will to achieve anything, no oceanic problem can hold you. This is a series of boulders, with a length of about 30 km extending far into the horizon.

In Christian mythology, this is Adam's bridge. According to legend, which is also given in Islamic texts, when Adam was expelled from heaven, he crossed this bridge, and then stood on one foot in penance on a mountain further south in Sri Lanka. After one thousand years of standing on Adam's peak, he was reunited with Eve.

In Indian mythology, it is Ram Setu, which was constructed by Hanuman and his band of dedicated followers to enable

Ram to cross to Lanka to rescue Sita. It can be seen clearly from Dhanuskodi, about 18 km from the main temple. The place (Dhanuskodi), once bustling now wears a deserted look due to a devastating cyclone in 1964, is named after Ram's bow. This is the place where Ram is said to have bathed before he worshipped his God Shiva. This is the place where Vibhishna surrendered to Ram. The temple constructed at the site is the only structure that survived the devastating cyclone of 1964.

The Pot of Nectar

Though Kumbakonam is the place where Murugan instructed Shiva on the meaning of the word OHM, the place has its meaning and sanctity attached to a different myth. As per that legend, after the end of each era, the whole world immerses in a deluge on account of the wrath of Hindu God Shiva for the sins committed by humans on earth. Brahma, the God of creation, recreated the world during the start of current Kaliyuga. Shiva declared that after the end of the previous era, a divine pot would reach a holy spot. As the holy pot reached the designated place, Shiva in the form of a hunter, shattered the cosmic pot (Kumbha) containing the divine nectar of creation (Amrit) with his arrow.

It is believed that when the divine nectar emerged from the pot, it filled the huge Mahamaham tank. This is Kumbakonam's sacred centre and the site of the great Mahamaham festival, held every 12 years when Jupiter and Moon are placed together opposite the Sun. The festival was celebrated on 8th March 2020 (Tamil month of Masi) recently.

At the auspicious time, thousands of devotees enter the tank for their holy dip. This is when the purifying power of the water is said to be at its height. The devotees believe that all of India's nine sacred rivers also bathe in the tank to cleanse themselves of the sins of humanity accumulated in their waters.

Purification of God

Suchindram is a small temple town that is 13 km from Kanyakumari. Its unique Sthanumalaya Temple (a temple of musical pillars) is dedicated to the Hindu Trinity of Brahma, Vishnu, and Shiva – all worshipped in the form of lingas though Vishnu is the main deity in the form of Dattatreya.

Dattatreya was the son of sage Atri and Anusuya, a pious and pativrata lady who always practised austerities and devotion. This allowed her to attain miraculous power. When the sage Narada told her qualities to the famous Trinity, they decided to put her to the test.

It was here they appeared to Anusuya as Brahmans and made a preposterous demand that they should be fed by her with her clothes removed. Anusuya, being pious, couldn't deny it. This was a challenge to her being a pativrata lady. To overcome this sort of situation she used her miraculous power and converted them into three babies and then fed them with the condition fulfilled. When the sage Narada informed their status to their wives, they rushed to Anusuya and asked to forgive their husbands, disclosing their true identity.

When the Trinity returned to their normal forms, they granted her a boon. She requested that all of them be born to her. So, Brahma was born as Chandra, Vishnu as Dattatreya, and Shiva as Durvasa.

Suchindram is also associated with the purification of the God Indra, after the sage Gautama had cursed Indra to be a eunuch, when he was found misbehaving with his wife Ahalya in his absence, in his disguise.

The Diamond-shaped God

Palani is just 20 km away from Kodaikanal. Palani, besides being more natural than Kodaikanal, is famous for its Subramanyam Temple. The image there is made of medicinal herbs, mixed to create a wax-like substance, thus said to have healing properties.

Subramanyam is another name of Karttikeya, the younger son of Shiva, born in order to destroy the asura, namely Sura and Taraka. Amravati is the place where Indra, by severe penance, induced Shiva to promise that a God of war should be born and be the deliverer from the tyrant Sura.

Shiva was at that time in meditation after the death of Sati at the Yagna ceremony of Daksha. Shiva then generated a vivifying principle and cast into Agni, who unable to retain it cast into Ganga. The child, thus being born on the banks of this river, was nursed by six nymphs, called the Krittikas – six stars that make up the Pleiades and were the wives of the sage-stars who constitute the constellation Ursa Major – who each called him her son, and offered her breast.

Skanda (Sanskrit "attacker") thus got another name Karttikeya. To satisfy them all, the child assumed to himself six mouths and received nurture from each. When Parvati saw the children, she was so transported by their beauty, and embraced all of them together so forcibly, that their six bodies became one, while their six heads and 12 arms remained, thus originated Subramanyam (diamond-like). He was born for the purpose of destroying Taraka, a Daitya, whose austerities had made him formidable to the gods. He is represented riding on a peacock called Paravani.

Fed by six mothers, he was really a God of war, who led the armies of the gods to defeat Taraka and Sura. According to the myth when he planted his spear in the earth, none could budge it save the God Vishnu. But he was defeated by his younger brother Ganesha in a competition to travel around the world to decide who would marry first.

While Subramanyam set off on his peacock to circumnavigate the world, Ganesha being intelligent enough just walked around his parents, saying that to him they were the world. Ganesha was married first and Subramanyam being unhappy, came to Palani disguised as a mendicant. Popularly known here as Dandavyuhapani (bearer of the staff) he is depicted in the temple with a clean-shaven head, holding a stick. During the Thaipoonam festival in the month of Jan/Feb, the temple attracts thousands of pilgrims, many of whom shave their heads as an act of worship.

He is described in the Sangam literature as a God of Kurunji because of his association with these flowers. While in the north, Kartikeya is usually considered unmarried, in the south, he has two wives, Devayanai and Valli.

Paradise on Earth

Hyderabad was founded by the Qutb Shahi Sultans of Golconda, under whom the kingdom of Golconda attained a position of importance second only to that of the Mughal Empire to the north. The old fortress town of Golconda had proved inadequate as the kingdom's capital, and so about 1591 Muhammed Quli Qutub Shah, the 5th of the Qutb Shah, built a new city called Hyderabad on the east bank of the Musi river by his chief minister Mir Mohammad Momin, a short distance from old Golconda.

Hyderabad, the 6th largest city in India, was planned as a grid with Charminar at its centre. The centre marks the spot where he first saw his lover, the beautiful Hindu dancer Bhagmati. The city was designed by architects from Persia. The architects also filled the city with green gardens designed to replicate heaven on earth. Thanks to its design and dominance of the Shi'i sect it felt much more like a Persian city.

The Sultan also had his palace built to be a recreation of the Garden of Eden. But Muhammed Quli named the city not for Paradise but for his favourite wife Bhagmati who received the title Hyder Mahal – Lion Palace. Hyderabad was known for its beauty and affluence, but that glory lasted only as long as the Qutb Shahi dynasty.

The Page Behind the Rage

Time was ripe. Irwin, who was more disposed to be friendly to the Indians than all his predecessors, was the Viceroy of India. Irwin was taking great pains to find the solution for the Indian problem; in England, the Labour Government was in power, a government that wanted to accede to Indian wishes.

British politics in those days was disturbed by continuous crises. Some hidden forces were working in England which wanted to raise the prestige of England, which had gone down as a result of the World War I. British PM Macdonald had declared his intentions to give more than what was required to transfer the power. The only question was not whether Dominion status should be granted, but when it should be granted, as the British could find no Indian politician to whom power could be transferred, Gandhi, having declined to accept a government post.

After the death of C R Das, a political vacuum was created followed by a period of disillusionment and uncertainty. Gandhi wanted a practical politician who could be trusted to act according to his own. His choice fell upon the younger Nehru, but the difficulty was that Jawaharlal, along with Subhash Bose, had founded a league which demanded complete severance while Gandhi was satisfied with Dominion status. So the British decided to adopt a 'step by step' policy and on the advice of Irwin, a committee of seven persons was formed whose personnel were confined to the members of Parliament only, which included no Indian.

The committee was headed by Sir John Simon and had Burnham, Strathcona, Lane-Fox, Cadogan, Attlee, and Vernon Hartshorn as its members. The purpose of the commission was to examine how far the essential conditions for responsible government existed in India. To avoid the summer of India, it made two visits to the country. In the first visit which lasted from February 3 to March 31, 1928, its main task was to examine the papers which the Government of India had prepared on the various aspects of the system of government in India. It was the second tour of the committee which began on October 11, and which had to meet the various sections of people, which was greeted with boycott wherever it went. Although the boycott was planned, the immediate cause of aggravation was the fall in the world prices of raw products which India exported.

In the Industrial sector also the effect of the rise of prices of articles imported from abroad was to increase the burden of the working class whose wages lagged behind the price increase. It was due to these conditions that there was at this time a recrudescence of the terrorist movement.

The boycott was so effective that the commission had to be sneaked from the railway station to their place of residence. The police had to protect them from being mobbed and to cordon off the demonstrators on the routes. The excessive zeal of the police led to unwholesome and even brutal incidents, for the crowds were pushed back by force and charged with lathis.

One such incident occurred at Lahore on October 30, 1928, which took the life of Lala Lajpat Rai, which was not only condemned but immediate revenge was taken just 2 months after by the murder of Assistant Superintendent of Police of Lahore, Saunders, by Bhagat Singh. And when the Simon Commission visited the Central Parliament in April 1929, a bomb was thrown in the Legislative assembly by Bhagat Singh and his associates. They were caught, taken to gallows, tried, and hanged till death on 23rd March 1931 at 7.30 pm in the Lahore jail.

The Impetuous God

In the Rigveda, desire is said to have been the first movement that arose in the One after it had come into life through the power of fervour or abstraction. This Kama, or desire, not of sexual enjoyment, but of good in general is celebrated in a curious hymn of the Atharvaveda, which exalts the Kama into a supreme God and Creator.

This Hindu God is one of the most pleasing creations of Hindu fiction. Different scriptures maintain different stories of his birth. According to one, he is the son of Vishnu or Krishna by Lakshmi, who is then called Rukmini, while others say he is the son of Dharamdeva by his wife Shraddha. According to another account he was first produced in the heart of Brahma, and coming out in the form of a beautiful female, was looked upon by Brahma with amorous emotions. He is sometimes identified with Agni or to be self-existent, and therefore Aja, 'unborn'. He is depicted as a handsome young man with a parrot as his vehicle. Apsaras surround him, and one of them holds his banner with his emblem, Jalarupa, a fish or Makara on a red background. His bow is made of flowers or sugarcane, his bowstring consists of a line of bees, and each arrow is tipped with a flower.

Kamadeva's arrows strike the hearts of people and cause them to fall in love. Endeavouring to influence Shiva with a passion of love for his wife Parvati, he discharged an arrow at him, but Shiva, enraged at the attempt reduced him to ashes, by a beam of fire darted from his central eye. When Kama was killed, his wife Rati was filled with grief but was informed by the goddess Mahadevi that Kama would be reborn and that she would again be his wife.

Meanwhile, Rukmini was longing for a child, and Krishna after being blessed by the Rishis Nara and Narayana, went to Mt. Kailasha and asked Shiva for a child. Thus, Kamadeva was reborn as Pradyumna. This is the myth behind Holi played in South India, where this festival is in honour of Kamadeva whose effigy is consigned to the flames.

Love Above

"For God so loved the world, that he gave his only begotten Son, that whatsoever believeth in him should not perish, but have everlasting life", according to the Gospel of John 3:16 (Ist century AD).

The idea of God exists is perfectly reasonable. The idea that the universe is a divine creation is intellectually demanding, but not impossible. The further idea, however, that God should take an abiding interest in the creation and especially in some particular part of it seems rather speculative. Many Greek thinkers of the Classical era ignored or repudiated it. The claim that God's interest is focused on a particular part of creation, namely humankind, seems suspiciously self-centred.

The starting point of the thinking which led to the idea of a God of love was raised by the ancient Jewish doctrine of creation. Late in the axial age, some Jewish groups reverted to the idea of divine love in an effort to redefine God.

The identification of God with love, which was enthusiastically taken up by Christ and his followers, was emotionally satisfying – a powerful, spiritual, creative emotion.

Christ's sacrifice on the cross, to "wash away" the sins of humankind, is a token to be the ultimate proof of God's love. Good Friday commemorates this crucifixion of Jesus

Christ, who died to save the world. The incident has been beautifully described In New Testament. It consists of four books describing the life of Jesus – the Gospels of Matthews, Mark, Luke, and John. The details of the crucifixion are in the 19th Gospels of John in 42 paras:

...[T]hen Pilate, therefore, took Jesus and scourged Him. And the soldiers platted a crown of thorns and put it on His head, and they put on Him a purple robe. He brought Jesus forth and sat down in the judgement seat in a place that is called the Pavement, but in the Hebrew, Gabbatha.

And it was the preparation of the Passover, and about the sixth hour: and he said unto the Jews, "Behold your King!"

But they cried out, "Away with him, away with him, crucify him".

Pilate said unto them, "Shall I crucify your King?"

The chief priests answered, "We have no king but Caesar".

Then he delivered Him to them to be crucified. And they took Jesus and led Him away. And He bearing His cross went forth into a place called the place of a skull, which is called in the Hebrew Golgotha. After this, Jesus knowing that all things were now accomplished, that the scripture might be fulfilled, said, "I thirst". Now there was set a vessel full of vinegar: and they filled a sponge with vinegar, and put it upon hyssop, and put it to his mouth. When Jesus, therefore, had received the vinegar, he said, "It is finished" and He bowed His head and gave up His spirit....

The City of Odds and Evens

Delhi takes its pride in being the capital city of India. It has maintained its status since medieval times. According to legend, Delhi was named for Raja Dhilu, a king who reigned in the region in the 1st century BCE. Proper lore holds that the city changed its locality a total of seven times between 3000 BCE and the 17th century CE, although some authorities, who take smaller towns and strongholds into account, claim it changed its site as many as 15 times.

Delhi has its advantage of being the administrative centre right from the Delhi Sultanate till date except for some brief periods, which Delhiites can't give a miss. Delhi was traditionally the emperor's city. First, the Sultans built the forts and then the settlements grew around them like Qila Rai Pithora by Prithvi Raj Chauhan, Siri by Alauddin Khiljji, Tughluqabad by Ghiyassudin Tughlaq, Jahanpanah by Muhammed Tughlaq, Ferozabad by Firoz Shah Tughlaq, Dinpanah by Humayun, and Shahjahanabad by Shahjahan.

Out of them, only Muhammed Tughlaq was audacious enough to take a decision to transfer his capital from Delhi to Devagiri, which he later renamed Daulatabad. Muhammed's decision to shift his residence to Devagiri would have been quite upsetting to the people of Delhi, for the royal court was the very heart of Delhi, and its transfer from there would have been rendered the city lifeless.

The people of Delhi had therefore good reason to resent the Sultan's decision, and they seem to have expressed their feelings about it by writing abusive anonymous letters to him and throwing them into the audience hall at night for the fear of reprisals, but even that boomeranged. Muhammed meant to do good to flourish a new city like Delhi was. But it was good in him that fuelled and fanned the flames of the fiend in him – he turned devilish to punish the people who failed to appreciate the good in him. Thus, when he found the missives reviling and insulting him, he decided to lay Delhi in ruins.

Having bought from all the inhabitants their houses, he commanded them to move to Daulatabad. A crier was sent around the city to proclaim that no one should remain in the city after three nights. To ensure this, he ordered a search to be made for any persons remaining in the town. And when his slaves found a blind man in the streets, he commanded that the blind man be dragged from Delhi to Daulatabad, a distance of 40 days' journey. He (the blind man) fell to pieces on the road, and of him, all that reached was his leg. This created panic and the city became deserted. The people who for many generations had been the inhabitants of Delhi were broken-hearted.

Daulatabad remained the capital of the Sultanate for eight years. When Muhammed finally gave permission to the migrants to return to Delhi, not a thousandth part of the original population of Delhi remained.

When the British decided to shift their administrative base from the port town to any other location, they had the medieval Indian history in their mind. Delhi, with its strategic location along the north-south, east-west route was their choice as a focal position to rule over the country, but the old emperor's Delhi was not suitable for their living conditions. So, they built New Delhi in the 1930s as their imperial capital. Raisina hill commanding a view of the entire area stood above 50 feet above the plain, but the top 20 feet blasted off to make a level plateau for the major government buildings.

While building it, their vision drew on images from both the English Garden city and the American city beautiful. On the one hand, imperial power wanted a tightly knit, high-density city with broad boulevards and large imposing buildings. On the other hand, the British felt that in hot and humid India they must have space, greenery, and low-density. Low bungalows on spacious parcels of land also ensured some distance between the British and Indians, an objective of imperial policy under crown rule following the Mutiny.

After the violent partition of India and Pakistan in 1947, the influx of millions of refugees from West Punjab in search of a new life radically transformed the imperial city's character. Especially after 1947, Delhi very rapidly turned into a city of migrants as it became firmly entrenched as the political and administrative centre of Independent India to which populations began to gravitate from other parts of the country.

In this melee, the original population was reduced to negligible in comparison to the outsiders. The family of one of India's former vice-presidents, Hamid Ansari, in old Delhi is one of the original Delhiites. Late Sheila Dikshit former Chief Minister of Delhi, while announcing the tagline Dildaar for Delhi had rightly said, "From the days of Mughals to the British and now, Delhi accepts everyone, and this is the city's biggest identity".

Jai Hanuman Gyan Gun Sagar

This is the line Hanuman Chalisa starts with. But nowhere in Ramayana have we found this quality of Hanuman much utilized. Even Hanuman had no inkling about it. We find him powerful enough that when he didn't identify Sanjivani, he carried the entire mountain with him. He was devoted to his lord so much that when he found Sita having applied sindoor for Ram, he rubbed the vermillion on his entire body. He had strong willpower that whenever any challenge was faced, he was called in to overcome it.

But very few know that he was also writing the story of Ramayana as it went. In fact, he was writing it on the rocks. Valmiki saw it and anticipated that the greater beauty of its style would throw his Ramayana into the shade. When he complained to the monkey the latter had so little of the author about him, that he told the bard to cast the verses into the sea. Valmiki obeyed the injunction and the beautiful creation remained for ages under the waves till the time of Raja Bhoja. It was during his reign that its portions were discovered. It was by his commands that Damodara Mishra arranged the fragments, filled up the chasms, and formed the whole into entire work, known as HANUMAN NATAKA.

He is also Yoga-Chara, from his power in magic or the healing art, and Rajata-Dyuti 'the brilliant'. Among his other accomplishments, Hanuman was a grammarian; and the Ramayana says, "The chief of monkeys is perfect; no one equals him in the sastras, in learning, and in ascertaining the sense of the scriptures. In all sciences, in the rules of austerity, he rivals the preceptor of the gods".

It is well known that Hanuman was the 9th author of grammar.

The Lifecycle of Mahabodhi Tree

Buddha Jayanti is celebrated on the day when Buddha was born. But according to the Buddhist texts, it is also the day when he attained enlightenment as well as the day when he attained Nirvana. Nirvana is a term normally used in Buddhism, indicating the blissful state of liberation from rebirth and the cycle of lives. So, it becomes imperative for us to know the lifecycle of that tree which helped Gautama Siddhartha or Sakyamuni to become Buddha.

As the story goes, the original Bodhi tree was cut down by Emperor Ashoka's wife because she was jealous of the time, he spent here at his Buddhist devotions. The emperor then revived the tree by nurturing its roots with gallons of milk and built a protective stone railing around it. The tree that stands today is said to come from the same stock as the original tree. Ashoka's son Mahinda took a sapling of the original tree to Sri Lanka on one of his proselytizing missions, the tree flourished there, and its sapling was later brought back to be planted at Bodh Gaya after the original tree had died.

Indian Gem Therapy

Gemstones are associated with nine heavenly bodies – the Sun, the Moon, the planets Mercury to Saturn, and the lunar nodes Rahu and Ketu. It has been laid down by Varahmihira in his Brihat Jataka as follows:

Ruby – Sun

Pearl – Moon

Emerald – Mercury

Diamond – Venus

Red Coral – Mars

Yellow Sapphire – Jupiter

Blue Sapphire – Saturn

Hessonite – Rahu

Cat's eye – Ketu

Together they make up Navratna or nine jewels, a term which has been in use from the golden age of the Gupta Empire when it was used to describe the nine leading talents of the Gupta court. This could be the era in which Gem Therapy originated.

Right Click, Taj

ASI has taken down the 'Gallery' section on the Taj home page. The 'Gallery' section had several pictures of the Taj Mahal in all its glory. But there was one discordant note while clicking on this link – the photos included an image of the interior dome of St Peter's Basilica complete with Latin inscriptions and frescoes by Renaissance artists. The confusion is nothing but natural. The figurative work done in the interiors of the Taj Mahal, which completes as well as contrasts the sheer whiteness of the Taj exterior, is no less artistic work done by Renaissance artists. In the 19th century, when the British captured Agra, the Taj Mahal's exquisite Parchinkari work struck them as decidedly non-Indian, so much so that they began to believe that it had been designed by a European artisan, working in consultation with the building's Persian and Turkish architects.

The local term for precious stone inlay is Parchinkari, meaning 'driven in'. In the west, it is called pietra dura, the Italian for 'hard stone'. In this art, minute slivers of precious and semi-precious stones were arranged in complex stylized floral designs set into a marble base. The technique had been honed by Florentine artisans in the late 16th century.

Widely circulated throughout Europe and the Ottoman empire, the technique is said to have been imported by

Emperor Jehangir in the early 17th century. Just as the artists of Akbar's royal atelier had studied and adopted the styles of Italian Renaissance painters, so did Mughal court artisans emulate and reimagine the techniques of Florentine pietra dura stoneworkers, while creating the world's beautiful monument TAJ MAHAL.

Ganga Jal

The Indian Government has launched a new initiative under which Indian post started delivering Ganga Jal at the resident's doorsteps. It is planning to tap an e-commerce platform for delivery of the same.

According to the Mahabharata, to chant the name of the Ganga brings purity, to see her assures prosperity, and to bathe in her provides salvation. Ganga has been explicitly mentioned in Rigveda by Samyu, the son of Brihaspati. Sindhuksit, the son of Priyamedha Angiresa also mentions the river Ganga in the Rigveda. Ganga comes from the folk etymology of Munda 'Gand' meaning river. The folk etymology would be a reduplication of root "gam/ga" i.e "moving-moving", "swiftly following", which only applies meaningfully to the river's upper course.

It descended on the earth with the help of Trinity. The Ganga, it is said, first flowed in heaven, from God Vishnu's toes. Bhagiratha, intent on bringing down the Ganges, persevered in a long course of austerities. After 1000 years, Brahma signified his pleasure and granted his request on the condition that he prevailed on Shiva to break the fall of the waters, else the earth would be washed away.

By further austerities, he propitiated Shiva, who commanded Ganga to descend and detained her in his hair. She wandered through his matted locks for some time until Bhagiratha engaged in further austerities. Shiva then discharged the water in seven streams, one of which followed the king, but in the way, she overflowed the place, where Jahnu was performing a sacrifice. Highly offended at this intrusion, he united the spirit of sacrifice with himself and drank up the river.

The gods and sages upon this came to him and appeased his indignation, and re-obtained Ganga in the capacity of his daughter when he loosed her waters from his ears, so Ganga is also known as Jahnavi. Such was the difficult process through which the Ganga came to earth, and if the Indian Government has taken care to deliver it at the doorsteps, it is not only imperative but also incumbent upon Indian residents to help it to de-pollute this sacred river to get the pure "Ganga Jal".

Encashment of Idea

Muhammed Ali was the most thrilling boxer ever, who won the heavyweight boxing championship three times. He was fast of fist and foot. He floated like a butterfly, stung like a bee. Even after his punches had taken their toll, his voice barely rose above a whisper. He was definitely the greatest. He fought in three different decades, finished with a record of 56 wins out of 61 clashes with 37 knockouts. Fearsome Sony Liston didn't go beyond the 7th round, he defeated the mighty George Foreman in the 8th round and nearly fought to the death with Joe Frazier in the 15th round.

In view of this, no one was expecting Chuck Wepner, a relatively unknown 30-to-1 underdog to stand before this 6'3" and 210 pounds personality in the ring. But Wepner did what no one thought he could do – he went 15 rounds with the world heavyweight champion. In the 9th round, he reached Ali's chin with a right hand, knocking the champion to the ground, shocking both Ali and his fans watching the fight. Wepner was only seconds away from being the world's heavyweight champion when his dreams were dashed to dust by the greatest in the rest six rounds on March 24, 1975.

Over a thousand miles away, a struggling actor watched the fight on a newly purchased television set. After watching Wepner whom most people didn't know, fighting the most well-known fighter of all time, all he thought was to write a script on what he saw that day. He began to write that night and 3 days later he had completed it. The script was converted into a film and it was he, who played the lead role of Wepner. The film Rocky, went on to win three Oscars, including one for best picture, thus began the multimillion-dollar movie career of one of the greatest actors, SYLVESTER STALLONE.

How Loud is the Sound?

There is much noise about air pollution, but nothing is on the air about noise pollution, which is also a silent killer.

The loudness (volume) of a sound depends on the energy of its sound waves. Loudness is measured on the decibel scale. Each rise of 10 decibels represents a ten-fold increase in sound energy. Big energetic waves move our eardrums a long way within the ear and sound loud.

The human ear is divided into three sections, the outer, the middle, and the inner ear. The outer ear consists of the auricle or pinna. The pinna is shaped to guide sound waves into the ear. The middle ear includes the eardrum stretched across the inner end of the auditory canal. Inside the drum lie three small bones, the hammer, anvil, and stirrup. They are not only small but the smallest bones in the human body.

Sound waves strike the eardrum and vibrate these smallest bones, which together modify and transfer the vibrations to the inner ear, where they are interpreted as sounds. So, the high-energy waves can cause damage to the low-powered bones. The upper limit is 85 decibels for 8 hours a day. Anything beyond that can cause non-auditory effects. Prolonged exposure to sounds of between 90 and 100 decibels can cause deafness. More than 115 decibels is injurious to the ear and more than 135 decibels can break eardrums. Newborns exposed to sound above 45 decibels may experience an increase in blood pressure, heart rate, respiratory rate, decreased oxygen saturation and increased caloric consumption. The World Health Organization also recommends noise levels of less than 35 decibels in hospital wards. So it can cause both auditory and non-auditory effects which include depression also.

The following are the sources and their sound energy (in decibel).

Low whisper – 10

Average whisper – 20

Quiet conversation – (20-50)

Normal speech – 50

Loud conversation – (50-65)

Traffic on a busy street – (65-70)

Train – (65-90)

Factory – (75-80)

Heavy traffic – 90

Thunder – (90-100)

Jet aircraft taking off – (110-140)

Space rocket lifting off – (140-190)

Nuclear explosion – More than 200

Father Who Played Mother First

Yuwandswa was the 25th of the line of Ikshwaku, of which Rama was 64th. He had many queens but no son, at which he was deeply grieved. He had the celebrated Munis of his kingdom instituted a religious rite to procure progeny. The Munis took several days to prepare a vessel of consecrated water and placed it upon the altar on the penultimate day. It still required some more mantras before the water could bear the desired fruit.

That night the king couldn't contain his excitement which was to come the next day. And when the sages had retired to repose, he stealthily crept into the sacred room where the rite was being organized, and in the eagerness to become a father he drank the water in the jar, which had been endowed with prolific efficacy by sacred texts.

When the Rishis arose and found that the water had been drunk, they hastily recited required mantras and blessed, "The queen that has drunk, this water will give birth to a mighty and valiant son". And in no time the Raja became pregnant. Now the question cropped up who would become a midwife to help him give birth. Indra consented to play the most wanted role and the king gave birth to a child from his right side. The sages then asked who would suckle the child, whereupon Indra offered his finger for the child to suck, and said, *"Mam ayam dhasyati"* (He shall suck me). These words were contracted, and the boy was named Mandhatri.

In Greek mythology, when Zeus, the King of the Gods, knew that he would be killed by his son born to Metis, the goddess of counsel, from him, he swallowed Metis while she was pregnant with Athena. She emerged full-grown from his forehead without a mother and Metis remained in the body of Zeus advising him from time to time. She was the favourite child of Zeus, so she decided not to have had neither consort nor offspring who would kill Zeus.

Breaking the Barriers

Wing Commander Anjali Singh has become the first woman in the country's military history to be posted in any Indian mission abroad. Such a post demands great determination. But Indian women have always proved themselves equal to men. They have broken the barriers for entry into some of the areas found unsuitable to them. They have been inducted even as the fighter pilots. Lt. Avani Chaturvedi became the first woman in India to fly a fighter aircraft solo. Mohana Singh became the first Indian woman to fly a Hawk aircraft. Bhawna Kanth has become the first day-time Indian woman fighter pilot. They have passed the endurance tests for this purpose which requires much strength and stamina.

There are other Indian women who have broken the barrier first in different fields. Some of whom we know because fields are distinguished, but some are unknown.

First chief election commissioner – Rama Devi

First judge of the Supreme Court – M Fatima Beevi

First to receive a gallantry award – Mitali Madhumita

First to receive Dhyan Chand Lifetime Achievement award – Aparna Ghosh

First to write an autobiography – Rasamundri Devi

First to go to study abroad and become a doctor – Anandibai Gopal Rao Joshi

First to fly an aircraft at age 21 – SarlaThakural

First to drive an autorickshaw – Shila Dawre

First to be an Indian Army Cadet – Priya Jhingan

First to fly solo as an IAF pilot – Harita Kaur Deol

First to pilot & captain Indian airliner – Durga Banerjee

First youngest to scale Mount Everest twice – Decky Dolma

First Air Vice Marshal and Air Marshal – P. Bandyopadhyay

First referee in Boxing – Rajia Shabnam

First commercial test pilot of the world – Capt. Surun Darsi and Capt. Rose Lapar

First to win a medal in Commonwealth games – Anil Ghiya and Kawal Thakur Singh (Badminton)

First to make hat-trick in football – Youlada-de-Suza

First degree of graduation – Kadambni Ganguli and Chandramukhi Bose

First barrister – Cornelia Sorabji (Allahabad High-court)

First to reach the North Pole – Pritisu Gupta

First to travel all around the world – Ujjawal Patil by boat

First Paratrooper of Indian Air Force – Geeta Ghosh

First to participate in the Olympic Games – Meri Lila Row (1952)

Across the Black Waters

Immigration to the UK has been one of the most crucial issues which powered the Brexit debate. Between 1990 and 2015, the UK's immigrant population more than doubled from 3.7 million to 8.5 million. India is the largest source of British immigration. Asians make up over 3.5% of the UK population – 20.8 lakh out of 5.8 cr. Of these Indian Diaspora constitutes 1.8% (10.5 lakh). London has the largest concentration of Indians (4.37 lakh).

Diaspora – the scattering or sowing of seeds, is a Greek word that was used most frequently to describe the exile of Jews from Judea in BC 586 by the Babylonians, and from Jerusalem in 136 AD by the Roman Empire. But the ancient Greeks used it to refer to citizens who migrated to a conquered land with the purpose of colonization to assimilate the territory into the empire. In the 20th century, the term has been used more loosely to describe the scattering of nationals and immigrants from any country across the world either due to persecution or for personal or economic advancement.

One of the earliest Diaspora of the last century involved Armenians who fled their Ottoman-controlled homeland at the turn of the 19th century. Jews and Armenians had long been considered the most successful Diaspora till the advent of the Indian Diaspora under different circumstances.

The first migrating Indians were probably gypsies, who were taken by Muslim invaders to first Afghanistan and Iran, and then moved towards Europe. In the south, Tamilians had been travelling for centuries to South-East Asia, settling in Sri Lanka among other places. The British colonization of India led to an Indian trickle because of England's slavery abolition act in the mid-nineteenth century, mostly in the form of indentured labour. The act left the plantation in many parts of the world devoid of slaves. In their place came a slightly more refined form of exploitation-indentured labour, a euphemism for slavery. Britain is home to more than four lakh Tamilians; nearly 3.5 lakh are Sri Lankans and the rest are from Tamil Nadu.

The two most prominent groups in the Indian Diaspora are the Punjabi Sikhs and the Gujarati Patels. Sikhs, considered among the most enterprising and nomadic of Indian communities, began emigrating in significant numbers during and between the World Wars in which they constituted a large number of British Indian troops. Much later, in the 1980s, large numbers of Sikh immigrants arrived in the UK, seeking political refuge from the traumatic events in Punjab. There is roughly 4.66 lakh Punjabis in the UK. The other important ethnic group in the Indian Diaspora, the Patels, flooded into Britain after many of them were expelled from Uganda by Idi Amin. Britain has an eight lakh strong population of Gujarati origin.

Britain left the European Union on January 31, 2020. This began a transition period that is set to end on December 31, 2020, with its concerns and expectations centred on jobs in Britain.

Spontaneous Revolution

More than 75 years have passed, when Indians specifically asked the British to quit. This was when Britishers asked Indians to join them in the Second World War with the same enthusiasm as that of shown in the First World War. But the volte-face by them after that had taught Indians a good lesson. Japan was approaching fast having already captured some important locations around the Indian Ocean.

Sir Stafford Cripps was on a mission to bring the Indian public round to the allied cause. Indians were agreed that the supreme command of the army and not administration should be in the hands of Britishers in wartime. But the Congress, without naming anybody as being suitable for the post, offered so much resistance that Churchill broke off the negotiations.

The failure of the Cripps Mission created for Gandhiji a moral crisis of a higher order. For him, the World War was a moral conflict – a struggle between democracy and dictatorship. He went into a thinking mode on his Monday of Silence. The solution that flashed was first communicated to Horace Alexander in a letter at the end of which he said, "My firm opinion is that the British should now leave India in an orderly manner".

Working on this concept, the All India Congress Committee in its meeting at Bombay on August 7, 1942, adopted a long resolution. The operative part of the resolution was, "The Committee resolves, therefore, to sanction for the vindication of the inalienable right to freedom and independence, the starting of a mass struggle on non-violent lines on the widest possible scale". Then on August 8, the Government of India issued a resolution that alleged that Congress was preparing for unlawful, dangerous, and violent activities. And before the draft of the resolution of the committee was discussed the very next day, the first blow fell. Early morning on Sunday, August 9 the police descended on the Birla House with arrest warrants for Gandhiji and his companions. Simultaneously all the members of the working committee in Bombay were taken into custody.

The powder magazine was there but the match was lit not by Gandhi, but by the Viceroy. As per the expectations of Maulana Abul Kalam Azad, then President of Congress, Gandhiji's directions to remain non-violent were disregarded by the leaderless masses and what followed was mayhem.

Undoubtedly, the 'Quit India' promoted the growth of the sense of national unity. The death of three to five thousand people and the arrest of more than a hundred thousand are proof of the participation of the masses. It was the greatest political danger to British rule since 1857.

Viceroy Linlithgow also reckoned it 'the most serious rebellion since 1857'. Given the warlike paranoia, he ordered massive repression, which involved the deployment of tens of thousands of troops, a like number of arrests, and perhaps a thousand deaths. The revolution was of little use to Congress compared to the earlier revolts, as most of their influential leaders were in jail.

One unfortunate effect of the 'Quit India' movement was that it divided the breach between Hindus and Muslims. In his resolution, Gandhi had made no mention of the Muslims at all. This made it easy for Jinnah to declare his neutrality as he had always picked up the pieces left by Congress and manoeuvred it to the use of his cause.

Jinnah who had retired to London in voluntary exile but was recalled in 1934 by the Muslim League which had sunk into insignificance. The Muslim League was founded in 1906 by the feudal landowners for the express purpose of protecting their class interests as they were afraid of the Congress and avoided it as a democratic body with socialistic interests. Thus, it had no influence on those Muslim circles that had no inherited landholdings.

This prominence gave Jinnah an aura of dictatorship in his party. Nobody dared contradict him. He opposed every form of democracy and every association with the public. He knew that his death was near. He was suffering from an illness of which he died soon after his triumph. He, therefore, pressed for a quick final solution. He wanted to show himself to the world as a head of state. Cripps mission was the first official recognition by London of the Pakistan idea as there was one clause added that the provinces should have the right to "opt-out of the Indian Federation".

The 'Quit India' movement was India's last great mass movement. After that, there were only negotiations. With the Congress leaders being in captivity, Jinnah was the only person with whom the Viceroy could negotiate, and this opportunity was welcomed. Jinnah used the religious motive which personally mattered little to him. His political ideas were influenced by those of Kemal Ataturk. He cared little for religion. He knew well enough that a state could not be founded on the basis of the Quran alone. But he was a clever tactician and was able to extort what he wanted from a British Government which was weakened by the Second World War.

On August 15, the British flag was hauled down, but, in Karachi, Independence was celebrated on August 14, so that Jinnah could create the impression that Independent India could comprise only the territory that was leftover. Jinnah, who did not know Urdu, read out the Proclamation of Independence in English and held out the thanksgiving service in a church, not in a mosque. Such is the irony of history!

The First Foreign Invasion

India got its Independence after many sacrifices not only in terms of loss of human lives but also in the reduction of its territorial extent. In reality, it was a consequence of the invasions that had begun around 1000 years back, invasions that subjected the larger part of the subcontinent to Muslim rule for hundreds of years. From several points of view, Muslim rule was as foreign as British rule. The largest territorial loss was West Pakistan – the old Indus Valley. This was the region that even in the days of Hindu rule had been ruled over by the adjoining Persians due to their commercial interests.

The history of the commercial relationship between India and Arabia was very amicable. There was however an irritant in this relationship, the menace of pirates operating out of Indian harbours, which hampered Arab shipping and trade. In one of such incidents, an Arab ship was captured by pirates off the port city of Debal in the Indus delta. The pirates not only plundered the ships but also seized Arab girls who were on it. The incident, particularly the capture of the girls, roused the wrath of Hajjaj, the pugnacious Arab Governor of Iraq.

He sent a missive to Dahar, the King of Sind, to arrange for the immediate release of girls. But Dahar, having no control over pirates, claimed that he was helpless to do anything in the matter. Hajjaj considered the reply evasive or deceitful. He then sent, with the Caliph's permission, a full-fledged army to invade Sind under 17-year-old Muhammad Qasim, his nephew, and son-in-law, who was then Governor of Shiraz in Persia. Heavy siege weapons were sent to Sind by sea, and this included a monstrously huge ballista ironically named 'Bride', which required some 500 men to operate it.

In June 712, Muhammad crossed the river and advanced on the fortress of Brahmanabad. where Dahar was stationed and was confronted by his huge army. But due to brilliantly innovative military tactics of Muhammed, Sind forces were defeated. Dahar's head was severed and sent to the Caliph as a trophy.

As the Arabs charged into the fortress, one of Dahar's queens committed Sati, but another, Rani Ladi surrendered and eventually married Muhammad. Two of Dahar's maiden daughters, Suryadevi and Pramaldevi, who were found in the fort, were sent by Muhammad to the Caliph, as a part of homage due to him.

History of Olympics

Greek mythology is full of stories of athletic games organized to mark the death of a warrior in battle. They also served as a ritual of cleansing for those who had killed someone. This was the hallmark of a masculine warrior society.

Mount Olympus is the place where Greek mythological heroes find a place. This is the home of Zeus, the King of Gods, and its residents are called Olympians. In a war spreading over 10 years Olympians led by Zeus had defeated Titans. According to legend, the first Games were organized among gods to celebrate this victory. During those Games, Apollo, the Sun God, beat Hermes, the messenger God, in the footrace, and Ares, the war God, in boxing. The games were revived by Pelops, the grandson of Zeus.

Pelops had defeated King Oenomaus of Pisa in a chariot race to win his daughter Hippodamia. Invincible Oenomaus had been deceived to be killed by felling off his chariot to the ground. To purify himself from the pollution that followed the killing of Oenomaus; Pelops revived the chariot games that had long ago been established by the Olympians to mark their victory over the Titans.

This was the year 776 BCE. Pelops renamed the old games as the Olympic Games. The land controlled by Pisa was called

Pisatis which included Olympia where the Olympic Games were held; and the island on which it stood came to be known as Peloponnese, the island of Pelops.

In the early centuries of the Olympic competition, all the contests took place on one day; later the Games were spread over four days. In most events, the athletes participated in the nude because ancient Greeks found nothing shameful about nudity, especially male nudity. There were no women's events in the ancient Olympics. The 2nd century CE traveller Pausanias wrote that women were banned from Olympia during the actual Games under penalty of death. However, he stated that unmarried women were allowed as Olympic spectators.

The supports for the competitions at Olympia and elsewhere fell off when Greece lost its Independence to Rome. The ancient Romans liked to play and tease people. Their term for the Olympic Games was 'Olympiorum Ludicrum'. Their Emperor Nero was somewhat a keen patron of the festivals in Greece, but he disgraced himself and the Olympic Games when he entered a chariot race, fell off his vehicle, and then declared himself the winner anyway. The Ancient Olympic Games were finally abolished about 400 CE by the Roman Emperor Theodosius I or his son because of the festival's Pagan associations.

It was none other than Pierre Baron de Coubertin who revived the Games once again. Due to only his efforts, Modern Olympic Games are being organized every four years since 1896.

The 2020 Summer Games that were scheduled to be held in Tokyo were postponed in response to the coronavirus pandemic. Now the Games will be organized in 2021, which will coincidentally also be the 125th year of its happening. In fact, the Olympics, by which we generally treat it to be as summer games, had never been smooth, in its 125 years of journey, except for one or two occasions.

1896 (Athens): 245 men from 14 countries participated. The athletes (all male) competed in 43 events. A crowd estimated at more than 60,000 attended the opening day of the competition. Members of the royal family of Greece were regular spectators over the 10 days of the competition. Hungary sent the only national team. The swimming events were held in the cold currents of the Bay of Zea. The marathon, conceived by Frenchman Michel Breal, was born, which was won by local hero Spiridon Louis. Most medals: German gymnast – Hermann Weingartner.

1900 (Paris): 1319 people from 22 countries competed. The second modern Olympic competition was relegated to a sideshow of the World Exhibition, which was being held in Paris in the summer of 1900. The Games suffered from poor organization and marketing, with events conducted over a period of five months in venues that often were inadequate. The track-and-field events were held on grass fields that were uneven and often wet. Broken telephone poles were used to make hurdles, and hammer throwers occasionally found their efforts stuck in a tree. The swimming events were held in the Seine River, whose strong currents carried athletes to unrealistically fast times. There was an infusion of new events, some of which were not officially part of the Olympic programme or were later discontinued. However, archery, football (soccer), rowing, and equestrian events were also among those introduced. Women competed for the first time. They participated in only sailing, lawn tennis, and golf. But the confusion prevailed over who was the first woman to win an Olympic gold medal due to mismanagement. Most medals: USA athlete – Irving Baxter.

1904 (St Louis): 687 competitors from 13 nations took part out of them 525 from the U.S. Like the 1900s Olympics in Paris, this Olympic took a secondary role. The Games originally were scheduled for Chicago, but the location was changed to St. Louis to combine it with the Louisiana Purchase Exhibition, a large fair celebrating the 100th anniversary of the U.S acquisition of the Louisiana Territory. The remoteness of St. Louis and growing tension in Europe over the Russo-Japanese War kept away many of the world's best athletes. Half of those who were outside the United States were from Canada. Some events included only Americans. Thomas Keily of Ireland, who paid his own fare to the Games rather than compete under the British flag, won the gold medal in an early version of the decathlon, in a single day. The swimming events took place in an artificial lake on the fairgrounds. Boxing made its Olympic debut. Most medals: U.S gymnast – Anton Helda.

1908 (London): 2035 men and women from 22 countries entered. The games were originally scheduled for Rome, but with Italy beset by organizational and financial problems, it was decided that the games should be moved to London. For the first time, an opening ceremony was organized. A running feud between an American and the British began when the American shot-putter Ralph Rose would not dip the U.S flag in salute to King Edward VIII. This refusal later became standard practice for U.S athletes in the opening parade. New events included diving, motorboating, indoor tennis, and field hockey. The games were marred by the allegations of bias by the British judges. The 400 metre final was nullified by officials who disqualified the apparent winner, American John Carpenter, for deliberately impeding the Path of Wyndham Halswelle of Great Britain. A new race was ordered, but the other qualifiers refused to run. Halswelle then won the gold in the only walkover in Olympic history. Most medals: U.S athlete – Mel Sheppard.

1912 (Stockholm): 2547 competitors from 28 countries took part. Known as the "Swedish Masterpiece" this Olympics were the best organized Games to that date. Electronic timing devices and a public address system were used for the first time. Swimming and modern pentathlon and diving events for women were included. The boxing competition was cancelled by the Swedish organizers who found the sport disagreeable. Most medals: Finland athlete – Hannes Kolehmainen.

1916: Games couldn't be organized due to the First World War.

1920 (Antwerp): 2669 competitors from 29 countries entered. The place was chosen in honour of the Belgian people, who had lived under enemy occupation and had been devastated during World War I. The defeated countries of World War I were not invited. The new Soviet Union chose not to attend. The city, plagued by bad weather and economic woes, had a very short time to clean up the rubble left by the war and construct new facilities for the games. The athletics stadium was unfinished when the games began, and athletes were housed in crowded rooms furnished with folding cots. The events were lightly attended, as few could afford tickets. In the final days, the stands were filled with schoolchildren who were given free admittance. The Olympic Flag was introduced. Most medals: U.S Shooter – Willis Lee.

1924 (Paris): 3092 people from 44 countries participated. Held in tribute to the Baron de Coubertin, the retiring president of the IOC and founder of the Olympic movements, the Games featured a high calibre of competition. Fencing was added to the women's events. The Olympic motto (Citius, Altius, Fortius) was coined. The first women athletes to represent India in the Olympics were N Polley and Sydney Jacob in tennis, singles, and doubles. Helen Wills of the United States won gold medals in the singles and doubles tennis events. After this, tennis was dropped from the Olympic competition because of questions over the amateur standing of many participants. The sport did not return to the Olympics until 1988. Most medals: Finland athlete – Ville Ritola.

1928 (Amsterdam): 3014 competitors from 46 countries took part. This was the first occasion that women competed in athletics events. Track-and-field and gymnastics events were added to the women's slate, despite much criticism by the Vatican. Controversy arose in the women's 800 metre run when several women collapsed from exhaustion at the end of the race; Olympic officials concluded that the distance was too long for women, and it was not until the 1960 games in Rome that women were allowed to compete in a race of more than

200 metre. Germany returned to the Olympic competition. The Games featured the debut of the Olympic flame. The dominance of America broke in running events, which won only three out of a possible 12 gold medals. Indian men's hockey team won gold for the first time. Most medals: Swiss gymnast – Georges Miez.

1932 (Los Angeles, California): 1408 people from 37 nations competed. Poor participation was the result of the worldwide economic depression and the expense of travelling to California. The Los Angeles Games featured the first Olympic Village, which was located in Baldwin Hills, a suburb of Los Angeles, and covered 321 acres. The male athletes were housed in more than 500 bungalows and had access to a hospital, a library, a post office, and 40 kitchens serving a variety of cuisines. The female athletes stayed at a downtown hotel. Uniform automatic timing and the photo-finish camera were used for the first time. Olympic rules allowed individual women to compete in no more than three games. Stella Walsh won a 100 metre women's gold. She was killed in 1980 during a robbery and an autopsy revealed that she was a man. The first race-walking event was held. Podiums for award ceremonies and the playing of the winner's national anthem were introduced. Most medals: Hungary gymnast – Istvan Pelle.

1936 (Berlin): 3738 competitors from 49 nations entered. The Games were held in a tense, politically charged atmosphere. The Nazi Party had risen to power in 1933, two years after Berlin was awarded the Games. Fearing a mass boycott, the IOC pressured the German government and received assurances that qualified Jewish athletes would be part of the German team and that the games would not be used to promote Nazi ideology. But only one athlete of Jewish descent was a member of the German team, and Reich Sports Field was draped in Nazi banners and symbols. Live coverage of the event was introduced. For the first time, games were preceded by the torch relay, which is transported from Greece. Adolf Hitler tried to turn the games into a Nazi propaganda event. The success of African American athletes like Jesse Owens, referred to as "black auxiliaries" by the Nazi press, was considered a particular blow to Hitler's Aryan ideals. Basketball and Canoeing debuted as an Olympic sport. Most medals: U.S athlete – Jesse Owens.

1940 & 1944: Games couldn't be held due to the Second World War.

1948 (London): 4099 people from 59 countries took part. Despite limited preparation time and after much debate when many countries were still recovering from the destruction of World War II, this Olympics proved a success. Once again, the defeated countries were not invited to participate. The Soviet Union also did not participate but Communist countries were involved for the first time. There was no Olympic Village; the male athletes were housed at an army camp in Uxbridge, while the women stayed in dormitories at Southlands College. The women's competition was extended to 10 events with the addition of the 200 metre run, the long jump, and the shot put. Most medals: Dutch athlete – Fanny Blankers-Koen (30-year-old mother of two children).

1952 (Helsinki): 4925 athletes from 69 nations entered. USSR competed for the first time (a Russian team last competed in the 1912 games). The Soviet Union announced plans to house its athletes in Leningrad and fly into Helsinki each day; these plans were dropped, but a separate Olympic Village for Eastern Bloc countries was created in Otaniemi. By the end of the competition, Soviet officials had opened their village to all athletes. Germany and Japan were allowed to take part in the competition. East Germany had applied for participation in the games but was denied. The games were so well organized that it was once thought to make it a permanent venue. Independent India sent its first women's representative that included Nilima Ghosh, Mary D'Souza, Dolly Nazir, and Arati Saha. Most medal: USSR gymnast – Maria Gorokhovskaya.

1956 (Melbourne): 3342 competitors from 72 nations participated. It was the first Olympics held in the Southern Hemisphere. Because of the reversal of the seasons, the games were celebrated in November and December. Egypt, Lebanon, and Iraq boycotted in protest of the Israeli invasion of the Sinai Peninsula in October. The Netherlands, Spain, and Switzerland boycotted in protest of the Soviet Union's invasion of Hungary to suppress a popular uprising against the government. East and West Germany competed as a single team, a practice that would last through the 1964 Games. Because of Australia's quarantine restrictions, the equestrian events were held in Stockholm during June. The Melbourne games introduced the practice of athletes marching into the closing ceremonies together, not segregated by a nation. The track-and-field competition was held at the Melbourne Cricket Ground. Most medals: USSR gymnast – Viktor Chukarin and Hungary gymnast – Agnes Keleti

1960 (Rome): 5348 athletes from 83 countries took part. The Games were the first to be fully covered by television. Several ancient sites were restored and used as venues. The Basilica of Constantine hosted the wrestling competition. The Baths of Caracalla provided the site of the gymnastic events. The marathon was run along the Appian Way and ended under the Arch of Constantine. Abebe Bikila became the first black African to win an Olympic gold medal. American Cassius Clay (later known as Muhammed Ali) first gained international attention as the light heavyweight boxing champion. This was the last game to which South Africa was invited for 32 years. Wilma Rudolph became the first American woman to win three golds in athletics in a single Olympic Games despite having a brace on her left leg due to a polio attack in her childhood. Milkha Singh was in a good second position in the 400-metre men's final. But in the final 200 metre stretches, he surprisingly slowed down, altering his pace to enable his competitors to overtake him, thus came fourth. Most medals: USSR gymnast – Boris Shaklin.

1964 (Tokyo): 5140 competitors from 93 countries participated. This Olympics introduced improved timing and scoring technologies, including the first use of computers to keep statistics. Before the Olympics, some players had participated in the Games of the New Emerging Forces. In 1963, the IOC declared that any athlete participating in that sports festival would be ineligible for the Olympics. A student born near Hiroshima on the day the atomic bomb fell lit the flame for the first games held in Asia. Most medals: USSR gymnast – Larissa Latynina.

1968 (Mexico City): 5531 people from 112 countries competed. The Games were the most politically charged Olympics since the 1936 Games in Berlin. Ten days before the Games were to open, students protesting the Mexican government's use of funds for the Olympics rather than for social programmes were surrounded in the Plaza of Three Cultures by the army and fired upon. More than 200 protestors were killed and over a thousand injured. Sprinters John Carlos and Tommie Smith gave black power salutes on the podium at the victory ceremony for the men's 200 metre run. Both athletes were banned from the Olympic Village and sent home. East and West Germany competed for the first time as separate countries. Drug testing and female gender verification were conducted for the first time. Most medals: USSR gymnast – Mikhail Voronin.

1972 (Munich): 7123 competitors from 121 countries entered. Tragedy struck when 11 members of the Israeli team were murdered by Palestinian terrorists. Nine other Israelis were held hostage as the terrorists bargained for the release of 200 Palestinian prisoners in Israel. All the hostages, five of their captors, and a West German policeman were slain in a failed rescue attempt. All competitions were suspended for a day while a memorial service for the victims was conducted at the Olympic Stadium. Archery returned to the Games for the first time since 1920, with events for both men and women. The basketball final was wrapped in controversy after game officials extended the contest by three seconds, allowing the Soviets the opportunity to score a final basket thus upsetting the United States for the first time. The U.S team, believing that the final result was unfair, did not attend the victory ceremony, refused their silver medals, and filed an official protest to no avail. Most medals: U.S swimmer – Mark Spitz.

1976 (Montreal): 6028 athletes from 82 countries competed. 26 countries, mostly from Africa, chose to boycott the Games when the IOC denied their request to ban New Zealand, whose national rugby team had recently toured apartheid-era South Africa. Questions arose about the integrity of the competition itself. Many athletes, particularly the East German women swimmers were suspected of using anabolic steroids to enhance their performance. Nadia Comaneci of Romania scored a perfect score of 10 seven times in gymnastics. Women competed in basketball and rowing for the first time. Poor planning and corruption meant that the games were a financial disaster. Most medals: USSR gymnast – Nikolai Andrianov.

1980 (Moscow): 5217 people from 80 countries took part. The Soviet invasion of Afghanistan in December 1979 led to the largest boycott in the history of the Olympic movement. Approximately 60 countries boycotted. Several of the participating countries refused to attend the opening ceremony, and the Olympic hymn was played at several medal ceremonies, rather than the appropriate national anthem. Despite boycott led by the U.S, Canada, West Germany, and Japan several world records were set. Indian hockey team returned with the prestigious gold medal. Most medals: USSR gymnast – Aleksandr Dityatin.

1984 (Los Angeles): 6797 athletes from 140 nations participated. A reverse boycott by the USSR, East Germany, and many other Communist countries, citing concerns over the safety of their athletes in what they considered a hostile and fiercely anti-Communist environment. China, however, participated in the Summer Games for the first time since 1952. The number of events for women grew to include cycling, rhythmic gymnastics, synchronized swimming, and several new track-and-field events, most notably the marathon. The games took place in the same stadium as in 1932. Romania's Cristina Cojocaru beat P. T. Usha to a bronze medal in 400 metre hurdles by 1/100th of a second. Such was the dramatic photo-finish that even the announcer handed the third place to Usha briefly, before correcting the decision in Cojocaru's favour. Most medals: Chinese gymnast – Li Ning.

1988 (Seoul): 8465 people from 159 nations competed. Violent student riots took place in Seoul in the months leading up to the Games. North Korea, still technically at war with South Korea, complained bitterly that it should have co-host status. Dissatisfied North Korea boycotted. Cuba and Ethiopia also stayed away in support of North Korea. Tennis returned to the Olympics after 1924. Table tennis and team archery events were also added. Ben Johnson won the 100 metre but was stripped of his gold three days later after testing positive for steroids. In all, 10 athletes were banned from the games for using performance-enhancing drugs. Most medals: U.S swimmer – Matt Biondi.

1992 (Barcelona): 9364 competitors from 169 countries took part. Soviet republics competed as the United team. A united German team took part. South Africa returned to the Olympic competition. This was the most successful Olympic event. The list of sports included badminton, baseball, and women's Judo. The Barcelona games were characterized by an increasing presence of professional athletes in the Olympic competition. Most conspicuous was the U.S men's basketball team, called the "Dream Team". Most medals: Vitaly Shcherbo for the United team.

1996 (Atlanta): 10744 competitors from 197 countries entered. Selected over Athens, Greece, to host the Centennial Summer Games, Atlanta staged one of the most extravagant Games in Olympic history. It started with a five-hour grand opening ceremony. For the first time, the Games received no governmental financial support. A bomb went off in the Centennial Olympic park killing one person. The perpetrator, American Eric Rudolph, was sentenced to life imprisonment in 2005. Hong Kong won its first (and last) gold medal before its reunification with China (1997). The number of events reached 271 as women's football, beach volleyball, lightweight rowing, women's softball, and mountain biking made their debuts. Most medals: Russian gymnast – Alexei Nemov.

2000 (Sydney): 10651 athletes (including three athletes from the United Nations dependency of East Timor) from 199 nations took part. Sydney was narrowly chosen over Beijing as the host city of the 2000 Olympics. The IOC was attracted to the city's long history of enthusiasm for sports. Despite some cost overruns and a ticket scandal, the preparations and the games themselves went smoothly. The high point of the opening ceremonies was Aboriginal Australian Cathy Freeman who lit the Olympic flame. She also thrilled the home crowd later on by winning the 400 metre. Several events were contested at the Olympics for the first time, including men's and women's tae kwon do, trampoline, triathlon, and synchronized diving. Other new women's events included weightlifting, modern pentathlon, and pole vault. Karnam Malleshwari became the first Indian woman to win a medal with a weightlifting bronze. Most medals: Russian gymnast – Alexei Nemov.

2004 (Athens): 10625 athletes competed for 201 countries. The Olympic Games returned to its birthplace in 2004. Doubts were raised in the media over security concerns, construction delays, high levels of air pollution. None of the expected calamities occurred. The world press raved about the success of the games as it apologized to Greece for its dire but groundless predictions. Women participated in freestyle wrestling and sabre fencing for the first time. A new medal was distributed replacing the long-standing design that incorrectly depicted the Roman Colosseum rather than a Greek venue. German kayaker Birgit Fischer became the first woman in any sport to win gold medals at six different Olympics, the first woman to win gold 24 years apart and the first person in Olympic history to win two or more medals in five different games. Rajyavardhan Singh Rathore became the first Indian sportsperson to win individual silver (men's double trap) since Norman Pritchard who won two silver medals at the 1900 Paris Olympics. The concluding event, the men's marathon, was won by Stefano Baldini of Italy after the leader, Brazil's Vanderlei Lima, was assaulted by a deranged spectator about 4 miles from the finish line. Lima, however, recovered to take the bronze. Most medals: U.S swimmer – Michael Phelps.

2008 (Beijing): 10942 athletes from 204 nations competed. In the months prior to the Games' start, a devastating earthquake rocked the Sichuan province. Nevertheless, China was determined to show the world, through an Olympic lens, that it had joined the ranks of the world's most modern and influential countries, and the games were considered a great success. The award-winning National Stadium (colloquially known as the Bird's Nest), designed by noted Swiss architects Jacques Herzog and Pierre De Meuron, was the centre of attraction. There were 43 world records and 132 Olympic records set. 86 countries won at least one medal at the games. That was the most first-place finishes at any single Olympic games. For the first time, the Indian men's field hockey team failed to qualify for the Olympics. Shooter Abhinav Bindra won the first-ever individual gold medal for India in the men's 10 metre air rifle shooting event. Most medals: U.S swimmer – Michael Phelps.

2012 (London): 10768 athletes from 204 countries participated. With hosting of this event London became the first city to organize modern games three times. It was a close finish in the selection, with London beating Paris (the heavy favourite, which also was attempting to become the first three-time host) by four votes. The opening ceremonies, devised by film director Danny Boyle, depicted the cultural and social history of Britain. The most notable addition to the London programme was women's boxing, which made its Olympic debut in three weight classes. Every participating country included female athletes. Saina Nehwal became the first Indian athlete to win Olympic bronze in badminton women's singles.

Sushil Kumar became the first Indian to win a back-to-back medal in the Olympics. It was India's most successful Olympic ever winning six medals (2 silver and four bronze). Michael Phelps became the most decorated Olympic athlete of all time, winning his 22nd medal. Most medals: U.S swimmer – Michael Phelps.

2016 (Rio): 10500 athletes from 206 countries took part in the fray. The buildup to the Rio Games was beset by more problems than any other recent Olympiad. Athletes, coaches, and tourists were wary of travelling to the crime-riddled city, where, also, an outbreak of the Zika virus led to the withdrawal of several prominent athletes. The waterways of the city were filled with debris and so polluted that the WHO suggested that athletes using the open waters avoid swallowing it, cover any exposed cuts with waterproof bandages, and shower as soon as they left the site. Fewer than 50 days before the Games started, the state of Rio de Janeiro declared a "state of public calamity", which gave authorities the ability to ration essential public services and made the state eligible for federal emergency funds. Despite all of these troubles, there were few significant problems during the currency of the games. Notable new sports that were added were golf and rugby sevens. One team of refugees led by Rose Nathike Lokonyen also competed under the Olympic banner for the first time. For the first time, the event was held in a South American country. Hanan Dacka, a 12-yr old Syrian refugee, jogged through the nation's capital with the Olympic flame in her hand. Two great athletes bided good-bye to the Olympics – Michael Phelps with 28 medals overall out of which six this time and Usain Bolt after completing triple-triple by winning 100 metre, 200 metre, 4 x 100 metre for the third time in a row. P V Sindhu became the first Indian woman to play an individual final for badminton and won silver for India. In other events, the home Brazilian men's football team won the first Olympic gold medal in the football-mad country's history on a dramatic penalty kick in the final by star forward Neymar. Most medals: U.S swimmer – Michael Phelps.

The Trump Card

The year 2020 is the 75th year when the first atomic bombs were dropped on Hiroshima and Nagasaki to end World War II. World War II was the most devastating war in history right from the beginning due to the development of science. When World War II began in 1939, air-forces had already replaced most of their fabric-skinned biplanes with all-metal, stressed-skinned monoplanes. Aircraft played a far greater role in military operations during World War II than ever before.

Bombers became larger and more powerful – converting from two to four engines in order to carry a heavier bomb load. The Hawker Tempest had a maximum speed of 700 kph and was one of the few allied aircrafts capable of catching the German jet-powered VT "flying bomb".

By 1944, Britain had introduced its first turbo-jet-powered aircraft, the Glossier Meteor fighter, and Germany had introduced the fastest fighter in the world, the turbojet-powered 'Me 262', which had a maximum speed of 868 kph. But the decisive factor was that of the U.S B-26 Flying Fortress that could carry up to 6.2 tonnes of bombs over a distance of about 3,200 km. This made the civilians more vulnerable to attack.

For the first time in warfare, more civilians than soldiers lost their lives. In total, more than 50 million people were killed. For the first time, the war was brought into the homes of people far away from the battlefield. The bombing of towns and cities meant that civilians became the targets of enemy action and often had to take refuge in shelters. The war, which lasted from 1939-45, involved every continent, and few countries (30 countries from five continents participated militarily), or people remained untouched by the carnage.

During 1940-41, the German air force bombed many British cities, and many civilians lost their lives. In February 1945, the Allied forces, consisting mainly of Britain and the United States, bombed Dresden, and more than 50,000 people were killed. This broke the backbone of the Axis powers, consisting mainly of Italy, Germany, and Japan.

Italy of Mussolini had already surrendered on September 3, 1944. Hitler, whose dictatorial powers and inflammatory speeches convinced many people that he could restore German pride and greatness lost after World War I, committed suicide, after Berlin fell on April 30, 1945. But the war against Japan seemed likely to continue as the Japanese fought hard to protect their country. The U.S plane B-26 commanded by Paul B Trigget dropped bombs on Hiroshima and Nagasaki to clear the last hurdle. Out of 300 scientists working on the project, only 19 were against it.

The idea of the project came, when in 1939 Albert Einstein brought to the attention of American President Roosevelt the destructive potential of nuclear fission – the principle behind the first atomic bomb. The U.S had not at this point joined the Second World War; nonetheless, Roosevelt gave the go-ahead to it. Los Alamos was approved as the site for the main atomic bomb scientific laboratory on Nov 25, 1942, by Brig. Gen. Leslie R Groves and physicist J Robert Oppenheimer, and was given the code name Project Y. The U.S had by now entered the war.

During the course of the war, the U.S presidentship changed hands and Harry S Truman became the next incumbent. Truman was the leader of front-line forces in World War I. He had seen the devastation from a very close end and was convinced that had the war continued for a few more days, he would not have survived. Two of his colleagues had lost their sons in World War II by now. He had four nephews in uniform.

On April 1, 12 days before he became president, the United States invaded Okinawa. The Americans considered Okinawa a dress rehearsal for the invasion of the Japanese home islands, for which the United States was finalizing a two-stage plan. The first phase was code-named Olympic, and the second Coronet. But in both cases, the mid-size casualties were estimated to be more than one lac U.S soldiers. It was disapproved by Truman.

Finally, at the Potsdam conference in Germany (which was defeated by then) in mid-July, Truman met with Winston Churchill and Joseph Stalin. It was when he received a report from Secretary of War Henry R Stimson that one bomb using Plutonium was successfully tested at a site in New Mexico. Truman shared this information with Churchill but didn't disclose to Stalin (who already knew it through one of the scientists working on it). The decisions of the Potsdam conference were conveyed to Japan, but the Prime minister of Japan Suzuki Kantaro dismissed the ultimatum, which didn't specify the use of the atomic bomb, well concealed by Truman, unlike his name. Ultimately, Truman decided to drop Little Boy on Hiroshima and Fat Man on Nagasaki to silence Japan, thus, dropping the curtain on Second World War. Douglas McArthur from the U.S was in charge of the ceremony in Tokyo Bay when Japan surrendered on September 2, 1945.

Albert Einstein and Enrico Fermi, who were involved in the production of the same atomic bomb in Germany in the 1920s, fled to the U.S to avoid Nazi persecution after Hitler took power in 1933. Bombarding was only possible through neutrons which was discovered by James Chadwick in 1932 only. The delay in discovery was probably a very good thing, as mastery of neutrons was essential to the development of the atomic bomb (because neutrons have no charge, they aren't repelled by the electric fields at the heart of an atom and thus could be fired like tiny torpedoes into an atomic nucleus, setting off the destructive forces known as fission).

Had the neutron been isolated in the 1920s atomic bomb would likely have been developed first by the Germans, which would have changed not only the fate of World War II but also the political structure of the world.

Once-in-a-Lifetime

An annular solar eclipse occurred on June 21, 2020. It lasted for six long hours. In this, the Sun looked like a ring of fire. A total solar eclipse can also last for many hours, but the totality cannot stand for more than 7.5 minutes. A total solar eclipse is a rarer phenomenon than an annular and partial eclipse.

A total eclipse happened on August 21, 2017, in the U.S was the first total solar eclipse to cross the country from coast to coast in 99 years. A total eclipse of the Sun, when in the middle of the day happens, darkness gradually descends making the brightest stars visible in the sky and is one of the most impressive dramas that the universe has to offer.

The fact that the Moon precisely covers the Sun's disc is simply a cosmic coincidence. Although the Sun is 400 times larger than the Moon, it is also 400 times further away from Earth, and it is this that makes both celestial bodies appear to be exactly the same size when viewed from Earth.

As already known, for a solar eclipse to be possible, the Moon has to be in the same direction as the Sun when viewed from Earth. That is, there has to be a new Moon. However, a solar eclipse doesn't occur every time there is a new Moon. That is because, relative to the Earth's orbit around the Sun, the Moon's orbit around the Earth is inclined at an angle.

Therefore, the Moon usually passes either above or below the Sun as seen from Earth. It can happen only twice a year and a total eclipse is even rarer, that comes once every 18 months and that too in a particular area.

There was no total eclipse in 2018. The next total solar eclipse took place on July 2, 2019, in the South of North America and West of South America. Another one will happen on December 14, 2020, in South Africa.

As Predicted

In a paper published in Nature, Google said it had achieved quantum supremacy and its computer performed a task that isn't possible with traditional computers. In this case, a mathematical calculation that the largest supercomputers could not complete in less than 10,000 years was done in 3 minutes 20 seconds. A proof that something is really possible even though it may be years before it can fulfil its potential. A proof that has been possible due to quantum mechanics, predicted long ago.

The physical elements of a computer, its hardware, are generally divided into its Central Processing Unit (CPU), main memory (RAM), and peripherals. The last class encompasses all sorts of input and output devices, keyboard, display monitor, printer, disc drives, network connections, scanners, and more. The CPU and RAM are integrated circuits – small silicon wafers, or chips, that contain thousands or millions of transistors that function as electrical switches.

In 1965 Gordon Moore, one of the founders of Intel, stated what has become known as Moore's law: The numbers of transistors on a chip doubles about every 18 months. Moore suggested that financial constraints would soon cause the law to break down, but it has been remarkably accurate for far longer than he first envisioned. It now applies that technical constraints may finally invalidate Moore's law since sometime between 2010 and 2020 transistors would have to consist of only a few atoms each, at which point the laws of quantum physics imply that they would cease to function reliably.

The Hierarchy of Stereotypes

The 2020 United States presidential election was scheduled on November 3, 2020. It was the 59th quadrennial presidential election for the 46th president. It is a paradox that the U.S had no female president till date despite claiming to be a free society with equal representation. The last election of 2016 was a near miss, which reminds us of the protests by the women thereat.

The day after what many had assumed would be the inauguration of the first female president, hundreds of thousands of women flooded the streets of Washington, and many more marched in cities across the country, in defiant, jubilant rallies against the man who defeated her. The marches were the kickoff for what their leaders hope will be a sustained campaign of protest in a polarized nation, riven by an election that raised unsettling questions about American values, out-of-touch elites, and barriers to women's ambitions. The march's origins were in the outrage and despair of many women after an election that placed gender in the spotlight as never before.

And why not? Because in the world order as it stands, those with power affect all our lives, for better or worse. The people who make decisions should be those who had experienced the world from their perspective. And no matter how rich or privileged a woman is, she still has a woman's body. Her perspective as a woman matters.

How, when, and whether we represent women matters. Negative representations instil women with 'stereotype threat', which means they perform badly in contexts where they are stereotyped as incompetent – not because they are incompetent, but because a portion of their brain is given over the desire to disprove that stereotype, rather than to focusing solely on the task at hand. Simply reminding women of their gender has been shown to impair their performance. Likewise, "impostor syndrome" has affected every successful woman i.e a woman can never quite believe her achievements are deserved. That she belongs at the top.

On the positive side, the palpable impact role models can have on a woman. They can influence her academic career choices; they can radically alter her knowledge of political candidates; and her likelihood of voting; they can transform her public speaking ability, enabling her to speak better, and for longer. By denying women access to the achievements of women who have gone before them, we are condemning them to keep having to leap over the same hurdles. Hilary Clinton was the perfect role model for them so her failure in crossing the last hurdle frustrated them.

This misrepresentation must stop. Can Americans break the mould of what it means to be a man and what it means to be a woman? Can they rebalance the hierarchy of stereotypes? In this election???!!! Certainly not. As Elizabeth Warren, who lost her candidacy to Joe Biden as Democrat representative, said so poignantly if American girls are looking for a role model in the Oval Office, they will have to wait for another four years.

From Panchsheel to Panchmantra

"Middle Kingdom" or "Central Country" is one of the most persistent names the Chinese have given their land. The 18th century Chinese world map demonstrates China's self-perception of its central position within a global setting. It conveys an unmistakable connotation of superiority, a vision of the world in which the barbarian rim is undeserving of the benefits and unrewarding of the bother of Chinese conquest. China constituted all the world that counted and the rest of humankind were barbarians clinging to the rim.

China was psychologically unprepared for the experience of the 19th century, when European superiority, first in war, then in wealth, became apparent. This was the period when the British had started acquiring territories in and around the Indian subcontinent, and finally, Queen Victoria was declared 'Empress of India' in 1858. China seemed stunned into backwardness, from which it is beginning to re-emerge today. All the border skirmishes with India are the repercussion of the same thought, the Galban valley is a recent example.

China had attacked Galban valley to stake its claim. The Chinese are now interpreting their perception of the LAC in a manner that seeks to redefine or maximize old claims along the new lines, as cartography and terrain knowledge has improved. For almost two and half millennia, they had aimed to unite all the new Chinese territories under one strong central power. They are habituated to receiving due respect from all other states.

Indian Prime Minister Narendra Modi in its first-ever India-China "informal summit" four years ago with the Chinese Premier had laid out his own five mantras which, he said, would now define the relationships between the countries and can be the building blocks of a future that emphasizes a convergence of interests.

The "positives" were Soch, Sampark, Sahyog, Sankalp, and Sapne. This reminds us of the period when Nehru paid a visit to New China which made a deep impression on him. Soon afterward in 1954, he entered into the first negotiation with China's great statesman Chou En-lai, who in the person of Nehru met India's most important representative. Nehru's readiness to abandon the privileges inherited from the British in exchange for China's signature under the Panchsheel sounded in Chou's ears like melodious wistful maxims.

Chinese statesmen believed their frontier with India to have changed to their disadvantage by British policy. So, it revealed to him that Nehru was evading a firm recognition of the frontiers. Naturally, the heady days were short-lived. Only a few months after the ratification of the first treaty between the two great Asian Powers, Chinese patrols began to feel their way on all fronts. Each encounter was followed by a diplomatic protest. Nevertheless, they were never made public so that for a while the Indian public did not know about it.

This the Chinese took as a hint to intensify their endeavours to push forward. But by early 1959, with a major Tibetan uprising having just been ruthlessly repressed, 100,000 refugees, pouring over the Himalayas, the non-Communist world up in arms, right-wing parties in India talking of Delhi's Buddhist betrayal and the Dalai Lama himself fleeing his homeland, the fraternal sloganeering froze in the thin Himalayan air. The dream of "Asian Solidarity" vanished.

By late 1959 both sides were tinkering with their border posts; clashes were being reported; Indian lives lost. There followed two years of recrimination masquerading as negotiation. This empire, under the leadership of the emperor and as the largest state in Asia, was habituated to receiving due respect from all other states. Therefore, the idea of taking India into partnership seemed abstruse. So, in mid-1962 the Chinese was tired of this game just as the Indians began to push their luck too far.

Chou En-lai chose the most favourable moment imaginable to invade India with four divisions which had been specially trained for months for a war in the mountains. Nehru now conceded that the nation faced 'what is in effect a Chinese invasion of India', the five principles of non-alignment had been flouted and nothing in my long political career has hurt me more.

Whether Panchsheel or Panchmantra, every maxim is futile for the Chinese statesmen. The only way of life that China adopted from India is Buddhism. Before that, there was very little contact between the two biggest powers in Asia. For a long time, relations between the two countries were maintained through Indian monks who carried the teaching of Buddha to China and through the Chinese who came to India on pilgrimage to the birthplace of the founder of their religion.

The Kushan rulers were the first around this area to establish political relations with China and soon found themselves on a warlike footing with China. The disputed area was the Tarim Basin. Emperor Wu Ti made the first attempt to annex that area from the Kushan rulers. This task was accomplished successfully by General Chang Kien. A Chinese by name Wang Mang, who revolted against the emperor, and usurped power over this territory, was responsible for its being lost again. 50 years later, Emperor Ming-Ti made another attempt. His General Pan Chao occupied the whole of the Tarim Basin.

The Kushans rose to defend themselves. Their ruler wanted first to raise his self-esteem by asserting his equality in rank with the emperor and asked for the hand of one of his daughters. The Chinese emperor took the proposal as a piece of impudence and had the Kushan envoy sent back in an insulting manner.

The Kushan ruler took to arms and sent a large cavalry force over the Tashkurgan Pass. This force was, however, worn out by its passage over the mountains, and was defeated by the Chinese under Emperor Hoti, near Kashgar. After that China was immersed in a period of internal confusion. Emperor Kanishka, the greatest Kushan ruler to take advantage of this, delivered a blow in revenge and brought Tarim Basin under his rule.

Then followed a long pause. Guptas had any diplomatic relations with China or not, cannot be confirmed. In any case, Guptas had no interest in the development of Central Asia. Nor did they take any more interest in the fact that Chinese troops had at that time again occupied the Tarim Basin. While the Guptas, by a last mighty effort, pushed back the Hephthalites, China became united politically under the Tang Dynasty and won back its 'western provinces', now called the Tarim Basin.

Emperor Hiuentsuang once more made an attempt to win back the Tarim Basin. But he now met with an entirely new opponent. The Arabs had arrived there. Emperor of China was defeated by the Arabs near the Tala river. This defeat compelled him to evacuate the larger part of his conquests in Central Asia. He was able, however, to keep the Tarim Basin, so that Sinkiang now became part of China. With that, there came an end of the first phase of political relations between India and China.

In the 13th century, China withdrew politically from Central Asia, as during this period the Mongols conquered its territory; and even when the Mongol rule had ceased, the Yuan Emperors avoided commitment in a region where the states of their tribal cousins lay. It was only when the Chinese dynasty Ming had ascended the throne in 1386 that China pushed forward again towards the Tarim Basin. But now those in power in Delhi were descendants of the Turks and had no interest in this region.

Empty Maps

Atal Bihari Vajpayee, former Prime Minister of India, once at the White House dinner on Sept 17, 2000, teased Clinton (former President of America), "I owe my presence here today principally to two persons, widely separated in time and also in space. One was the explorer, Christopher Columbus, who set sail for India but landed in America. I sometimes wonder where you would be, or where we would be if he had actually reached India." In fact, Columbus was the victim of a defective map of that time.

For thousands of years, the greatest thinkers and scholars had known only Europe, Africa, and Asia. Obviously, none of them really knew the whole of the world. Unfamiliar areas were simply left out or filled with imaginary monsters and wonders. These maps had no empty spaces. They gave the false impression of familiarity with the entire world. The crucial turning point came in 1492, when Christopher Columbus sailed westward from Spain, seeking a new route to East Asia mainly India. But he still believed in the old 'complete' world maps.

The size of the globe was worked out with remarkable accuracy by Eratosthenes, a librarian in Alexandria, around 200 BC, using a mixture of trigonometry, which was infallible, and measurement, which left room for doubt. Controversy over his findings remained academic, until Christopher Columbus, challenged them, nearly 1,700 years later.

He believed in two calculations, according to which the world seemed about 25 percent smaller than it really is. One was devised by the Greek philosopher Poseidonius, the teacher of the great Roman statesman Marcus Tullius Cicero. But Poseidonius could only guess the distance, and his calculation for the size of the Earth was less than three-quarters of what Eratosthenes had found. The Arab value also agreed with the value calculated by him or, so Columbus argued, ignoring or forgetting that the Arabs expressed their result in Arab miles, which were longer than the Roman miles with which Poseidon worked.

So, Columbus embarked on his journey believing that the Earth was just three-fourths of the Earth as measured by Eratosthenes assuring his backers that his small wooden ships could survive the journey. He persuaded the king and queen of Spain to finance his voyage.

Columbus himself never said the world was round – he thought it was pear-shaped and about a quarter of its actual size. His voyage of 1492 wasn't intended to discover a new continent but to prove that Asia was much closer than anyone imagined. He believed that only the Atlantic separated Europe from eastern Asia. His figures were all hopelessly wrong, but they convinced him that the ocean that lapped western Europe must be narrower than was generally believed. This was the basis of his belief that he could cross it.

Columbus had few instruments to help him navigate across the ocean. He used a cross-staff and astrolabe to calculate the ship's latitude, but he had no way of knowing its longitude. He was saved from disaster because an unexpected continent lay in his way.

On August 3, 1492, Columbus sailed from Palos with the Santa Maria, the Pinta, and the Nina. On October 12, 1492, at about 2 am, the Columbus expedition collided with the unknown continent. Juan Rodriguez Bermejo, watching from the mast of the ship Pinta, spotted an island, and shouted 'Land! Land!

Columbus believed he had reached a small island off the East Asian coast and called the people he found there 'Indians'. Actually, it was not even mainland America – it was the Bahamas. The next year, 1493, he came home saying, "Guys, there's a whole new world out there", He not only remained convinced to the end that he had reached the coast of Asia but made his crew swear an oath that, if asked, they would say they had reached India.

That mistake proved costly for Columbus. It was Amerigo Vespucci, an Italian sailor, who cleared the air over it. He took part in several expeditions to America in the years 1499-1504. Between 1502-1504, two texts describing these expeditions were published in Europe. They were attributed to Vespucci. These texts argued that the new lands discovered by Columbus were not islands of the East Asian Coast, but rather an entire continent unknown so far to Europe.

In 1507, convinced by these arguments, a respected mapmaker named Martin Waldseemüller published an updated world map, the first to show the place where Europe's westward sailing fleets had landed in a separate continent. Having drawn it, Waldseemüller had to give it a name. Erroneously believing that Amerigo Vespucci had been the person who discovered it, Weldsmiiller named the country in his honour – America.

Though Christopher Columbus, who was himself named after St. Christopher, the patron saint of travellers, couldn't give his name to the new continent, his journey has often been acclaimed as one of the greatest turning points in history. The consequences included the reversals of three great historical trends. The world balance of economic power, which had long favoured the Chinese, began gradually to shift in favour of western Europeans, once they got their hands on the resources and opportunities of the Americas.

Missionaries and migrants revolutionized the world balance of religious allegiance by making the New World largely Christian. Before, Christendom was a beleaguered corner; henceforth, Christianity became the biggest religion.

Festivals

Festival, also called feast, is the day or period of time set aside to commemorate, ritually celebrate, or re-enact, or anticipate events or seasons – agricultural, religious or sociocultural – that give meaning and cohesiveness to an individual and the religious, political, or socio-economic community. Because such days or periods generally originated in religious celebrations or ritual commemorations that usually included sacred community meals, they are called feasts or festivals.

The modern practice of vacations, i.e. periods in which persons are "renewed" or participate in activities of "recreations" is derived from the ancient Roman religious calendar in a reverse fashion. Days that were not considered sacred were called *dies vacantes*, vacant days, during which people worked.

In modern times, however, vacations are periods of rest, renewal, or recreation that may be sacred or secular holidays- or simply periods of time away from everyday work allowed by modern business or labour practices.

In 1953, when the first day of the lunar New Year coincided with a solar eclipse, the government of the People's Republic of China expressed anxiety that the repressed "religious popular superstitions" might encourage some form of antigovernment activity. According to the views of Confucious and Mencius, a solar eclipse during the New Year's festival is a sign of a coming disaster and a lack of favour by Shang Ti, the Heavenly Lord, who sends omens to indicate his disapproval of man's evil activities.

In Egyptian mythology, the Pharoh was believed to be the son of the Sun God Horus of the Horizon (Harakhte), symbolized by the falcon: the Sun God was also known as Re, among other names. The Sun God was also known as Atum, which means "to be at the end", or the west.

In Mesopotamia, on the occasion of New Year, The Enuma Elish, the epic of creation, was read at the New Year's festival in order to remind the participants that the cosmos arose out of chaos by means of a struggle between Marduk, the God of heaven, and Tiamat, the goddess of the deep and the powers of chaos. The New Year's festival was sometimes celebrated over a period of 10 to 12 days, in Babylon. On the 5th day, a ship was beheaded; the body of the sheep was thrown into the river, and the head was taken into the wilderness. Before the sunrise of the 3rd day following the scapegoat ceremony, the Babylonian king had to submit to ritual acts of humiliation; his symbols of power were removed, and the priest (Urigallu) hit him in the face. During the three days between the sacrifice of the sheep and the reinvestiture of the king, the populace of the city engaged in chaotic activities, perhaps of a carnival-like nature. On the 10th day, a banquet involving the king, priests, temple functionaries, and the gods was held to celebrate the renewal of nature, man, and society.

Dances by old women and sacrifices of live dogs (by throwing them down from the temple pyramid) were some of the activities that occurred during the Maya New Year's festival. Rogation festivities (Days of asking), originally held by the ancient Romans to counteract the effectiveness of the deity (Robigus) of red mildew on wheat, were reinterpreted by early medieval Christians of the West from the 5th century on as litanies for the blessing of the seed. Rogation Day, the 5th Sunday after Easter, is still practised in the 20th century in rural Roman Catholic, Anglican, and Lutheran churches.

Among the Kikuyu of eastern Africa, the mother and child symbolically die and rise again during and after a ceremony of seclusion, after which a feast is held in which a goat is sacrificed and prayers are said.

Among the Masai of eastern Africa, youths pass from childhood to adulthood by the rite of circumcision. After various preliminary activities, the boys (12 to 16 years of age) are circumcised and the blood released from the operation is later placed on their heads. After 4 days of seclusion and a period during which they are dressed in female attire, their heads are shaved, and they attain the status of adults and thus can become warriors.

Among the ancient Greeks, Thanatos (death) is the twin brother of Hypnos (sleep), and from this conceptual relationship may come the view that death is merely a sleeping stage in the passage from this life to an afterlife.

Secular modernist festivals are often mixed with previous religious festivals. May Day, once mainly a springtime fertility festival can be traced back to the Magna Mater (Great Mother) festivals of Hellenistic times, has become a festival of the labouring class in Socialist countries.

Of early origin, the Holi festival of Hinduism once a fertility festival, it incorporates a pole, similar to the Maypole of Europe, that may be a phallic symbol.

One of the best-known festivals of ancient Rome was the Saturnalia, a winter festival celebrated on December 17-24. December 25 – the birthday of Mithra, the Iranian God of light, and a day devoted to the invincible Sun, as well as the day after the Saturnalia was adopted by the church as Christmas, the nativity of Christ, to counteract the effects of these festivals.

The sacraments of the medieval Western Church lost some of their earlier interpretive values in the 16th century during the Reformation, and the month of fasting before the Feast of Bema (judge's seat) – a festival commemorating the death of Mani, a 3rd century AD Iranian prophet who founded the syncretistic Manichean religion-probably became the prototype of the Muslim fast month of Ramadan after Islamic invasions of the 7th century AD.

On November 1, Mexicans celebrate the Day of the Dead, to honour people who have died. Families have picnics by the graves of their relatives, decorate the street with flowers and carved skeletons, and eat sweets shaped like skulls and coffins.

To mark Children's Day (May 5) in Japan, streamers in the shape of carp are hung out. The strong energetic fish is seen as a good role model for young children.

On Christmas Eve, townspeople in Oaxaca, Mexico, celebrate their radish crop by carving large, recently harvested radishes into elaborate shapes, which they use to decorate their market stalls and restaurants. Food is served on chipped plates, which are saved for the occasion and smashed at night.

In England, people often used the last of the year's corn to make a figure called corn dolly. The dolly kept the corn-spirit alive through the winter, ensuring another good harvest the next year.

The famous Italian carnival first began in the 11th century. Traditionally, many revellers wear masks. They originally did this to hide their faces while they behaved outrageously.

In many Roman Catholic countries, Carnival is by tradition the last chance for merrymaking before the start of Lent, the weeks of fasting that come before Easter. Thousands of people enjoy the week-long Mardi Gras carnival in New Orleans, USA, which is named after the French for "Fat Tuesday". This refers to Shove Tuesday, the day before Lent begins when all the fats in the home must be used up. On this day they throw coloured paint upon each other for pastime, and upon anybody else walking in the street.

Second Spot

Prime Minister of India Narendra Modi, on August 5, 2020, participated in "Bhoomi Poojan" to start the building process of a grand Ram Temple at Ayodhya after a Supreme Court verdict. Ayodhya is the birthplace of the beloved God of the Hindus, Ram.

The birthplace of any God, as a human, is the sacred place for the concerned religionists. For Hindus, Ram and Krishna are the two incarnations of, one of the Trinity gods, Vishnu. Krishna was born at Mathura in jail, while Ram was born at Ayodhya in a palace.

According to Hindu mythology, Vishnu took his incarnations to perform extraordinary feats to save the order of the world. The feats were impossible for an ordinary human being. In order to achieve the same, they performed some God-like acts. Both of them left their birthplaces to save the world from the satanic disorders.

While for Krishna, to escape the jail some miraculous events took place like the doors of the prison opened one by one; ferocious guards were intoxicated into a deep slumber until dawn; the Nag worked as an umbrella to keep him from being drenched in a heavy downpour; the Yamuna kept her level below his feet dangling from the basket he was being carried in. This all proved right from his birth that he is nothing but an incarnation of Vishnu. He returned to his birthplace to kill his maternal uncle Kansa. So, he made his birthplace a workplace too.

Ram has no such pranks associated with his birth to prove such. He was as good as a human, when he left with Vishwamitra to kill, Tarika, the female demon. On the way he turned Ahalya from stone to human form, thus giving indications that he is an incarnation of Vishnu. But immediately after returning to his birthplace, he was exiled for 14 years on the orders of his father, who was provoked by his second wife, Kaikeyi, to do so. And when he finally returned to his birthplace, he only ruled as an ordinary human.

Tapovan in Nashik is the place where Rama spent his 14 valuable years of life as "Banvasi". The town of Nashik is one of India's holiest sites. A bustling temple town built on both banks of the Godavari river. It has almost 200 shrines. Ramakund, the centrally located tank, and the town's focal point is believed to mark the spot where Rama and his wife Sita bathed. The Kala Ram temple, east of Ramakund, is built in black stone with a 25 metre high shikhara. It supposedly marks the spot where Sita was abducted by Ravana (according to a version of Ramayana the Sita whom Ravan kidnaps is a pseudo-Sita, a phantom, while the real Sita is protected by Agni, the fire God), the turning point of Ramayan. Nashik has been named so because it is here that Lakshmana cut off the nose of Shurpnakha, the sister of Ravana. Nashik is the Sanskrit word meaning nose.

Nashik is a more important place than Ayodhya for a grand temple to build at because Rama behaved and acted like a God from here onwards till he killed Ravana. It is the workplace of Vishnu, incarnated as Rama.

OVER TO YOU

Index